Grasp cord and pull from wrapper

The New Museum of Contemporary Art, New York, New York

The MIT Press, Cambridge, Massachusetts; London England

Bad Girls

An exhibition organized by Marcia Tucker at The New Museum
of Contemporary Art, New York.
Part I: January 14 – February 27, 1994
Part II: March 5 – April 10, 1994

Bad Girls West

An independent sister exhibition organized by guest curator Marcia Tanner
for the UCLA Wight Art Gallery, Los Angeles.
January 25 - March 20, 1994

Catalogue ©1994 The New Museum of Contemporary Art, New York
"All That She Wants" ©1994 Linda Goode Bryant

Library of Congress Catalog Card Number: 93-87805
ISBN 0-262-70053-0

This catalogue has been organized by Mimi Young and Melissa Goldstein; edited by Tim Yohn;
designed by Susan Evans and Brian Sisco, Sisco & Evans, New York; and printed by Mercantile
Printing Company, Inc., Worcester, Massachusetts.

Bad Girls is made possible by a major grant from The Henry Luce Foundation, Inc. Generous
support was also provided by the New York State Council on the Arts, Penny McCall, and by
members of the Director's Council of The New Museum of Contemporary Art.

The "Zine" was made possible through the generosity of Arthur Goldberg.
Bad Girls logo by Nancy Dwyer.

Partial funding for *Bad Girls West* was provided by the UCLA Art Council, the UCLA School of
the Arts, the Kirkeby Foundation, and the California Arts Council.

The individual views expressed in the exhibition and publication are not necessarily
those of the Museum.

The New Museum of Contemporary Art,
583 Broadway, New York, New York 10012

The MIT Press, Massachusetts Institute of Technology,
55 Hayward Street, Cambridge, Massachusetts 02142

Bad Girls

Introduction and Acknowledgments

Marcia Tucker

Bad Girls has its genesis, for me, in an ongoing engagement with feminism, starting way back in 1968 when the Women's Movement hit New York. In recent years I began to see the work of an increasing number of artists who were dealing with feminist issues in new and refreshing ways, and the idea for an exhibition gathered momentum. The work that particularly fascinated me and pushed me to rethink a lot of old issues had two characteristics in common. It was funny, *really* funny, and it went "too far."

Word of the exhibition has provoked three main questions about it. The first and perhaps most difficult question I've been asked is, "Is this a feminist show?" Rumors of feminism's death in the mainstream press have been greatly exaggerated, I'm happy to say. My impression is that for the vast majority of younger women in the arts, feminist issues are paramount; look at the tremendous growth and energy of WAC (the Women's Action Coalition), which began less than two years ago, or the continued vitality and contentiousness of The Guerrilla Girls. Nonetheless, there are wildly differing ideas about what feminism is today, and it's difficult to arrive at any single definition of it, so much so that "feminisms" has become the descriptive term. What's more, some women who refuse the term categorically have attitudes, ideas and behavior that I would call entirely feminist, while others who describe themselves as such don't behave as if they are. As for the artists in the show, I haven't stipulated that they call themselves feminists; I'm sure there are some who do and some who don't, all for very different reasons.

But finally I want to frame *Bad Girls* through my own concerns and a lifelong engagement with feminism; this doesn't mean, though, that this is the only way of presenting some of the issues raised by the exhibition, nor is it the only way of seeing them.

The second question is: "Just what do you mean by 'Bad Girls'?" Forty-odd years ago, when my mother would mention that she was "going out to play Mah-Jong with the girls," she had no idea that "girls" over eighteen would one day be called "women," and between puberty and adulthood they would be referred to as "young women." It took 25 years for grown women to convince men that their use of the term "girl" was unacceptable to them, but by now the word again has positive connotations in certain circumstances. For example, when African-American women call each other "girl," it is a term of affection and familiarity. It has also been used frequently in music; like "sister acts" in the 1940s, "girl groups" were a fixture in 1950s *doo-wop*, and the term has now been revived for the young, tough, rebellious, independent women musicians who make up post-punk groups like Seattle's Riot Grrrls or the rappers in TLC.*

In entertainment slang, "bad" girls—originally appropriated from Black English to mean really good—describes female performers, musicians, actors and comedians (among them Bette Midler, Madonna, Sandra Bernhard, Roseanne Arnold, Lily Tomlin, Whoopi Goldberg, Paula Poundstone and Kate Clinton) who challenge audiences to see women as they have been, as they are, and as they want to be. In literature, well known and popular writers like Alice Walker, Angela Carter, Toni Morrison, Julia Alvarez, Amy Tan, Jeanette Winterson, and Cristina Garcia offer a refreshing antidote to such violent, tough-guy, misogynist writers as Norman Mailer and Bret Easton Ellis.

In the visual arts, increasing numbers of women artists, photographers, cartoonists, performers, video and filmmakers are defying the conventions and proprieties of traditional femininity to define themselves according to their own terms, their own pleasures, their own interests, in their own way. But they're doing it by using a delicious and outrageous sense of humor to make sure not only that everyone gets it, but to really give it to them as well. That's what we mean by "bad girls."

The third question most people ask is: "Why did you include men in the show?" Besides wanting to transgress the usual premise for an exhibition about feminist issues—that it contains only the work of women—we're not interested in reinforcing a separate category of "women's art," nor do we insist on women's concerns being inherently different from those of men, no matter how fed up with some of the latter we might be. But there are difficulties in including the work of men in this kind of exhibition, which is why there are so few of them in it. One of the artists, Cary Leibowitz, even pointed out that nowadays most men who are making art about gender issues are

---

*Says 21 year-old Candice Pederson, head of K Records in Seattle, "When women do something for themselves, it's construed as being anti-male. Well, if we have to go through five years of reverse sexism so we can have the same thing that men have, that doesn't compare to 2,000 years of sexism against women." Quoted in Linda Keene, "Feminist Fury," *The Seattle Times/Seattle Post-Intelligencer,* March 21, 1993, p. 15.

really trying to be good boys rather than bad girls. From my own perspective, the historic battle for women's rights hasn't become any easier, although it has evolved in more complex ways, but it seems counterproductive to turn away willing soldiers because of their gender, much less their age, race or class. They might have a different fighting style, but so what?

The history of the artist as "bad girl" is a long and—for women, at least—venerable one, but these foremothers weren't described as "bad" until quite recently; they were just ignored. Their legacy, however, is clearly present in the work in this exhibition, as Marcia Tanner eloquently demonstrates in her catalogue essay. Nonetheless, neither of us would have attempted to make this a historical exhibition, even had we been able to do so with the vast amount of ground to be covered. Instead, we've tried to provide viewers with an idea of the current scope and breadth of this kind of work—a kind of Whitman's Art Sampler—in the hope that the exhibition will open out onto this vast terrain, rather than close it off by trying to be definitive. And because so much of this artistic activity is inseparable from and informed by popular culture, I've included music, television, cartoons and comic books, fictional and other writing, and the work of children in the New York show.

There are too many artists in the two exhibitions to be able to discuss the work of each individually, so I've chosen to frame my discussion of *Bad Girls* more generally, outlining three main concerns: the importance of self-representation in effecting change in the status of women, and the use of humor as an essential component of it; the potential of recent analyses of carnival and the carnivalesque to shed light on contemporary feminist activity in the arts; and the role of popular culture and the mass media in shaping this activity. These are complex topics which are being widely discussed across academic and artistic disciplines. What I am trying to do here is to point to new and continuously changing relationships within these broad areas, and to show how the kind of work in *Bad Girls* might help us to see and understand a gendered world from a different perspective.

* * * *

One of feminism's greatest legacies for me personally is experiencing the pleasure of collaboration with others, especially those whose outlook is different from my own. This exhibition is the result of many such collaborations, for which I am deeply grateful. Marcia Tanner and I initially discussed the idea of an exhibition of this kind, and while it started as a small, informal, "what-if" project, it grew like kudzu into the present independently organized sister exhibitions which have three parts, two venues and one catalogue, and as Marcia recently said, still cries out for more. (*Daughter of Bad Girls*, Part XIV?) I'm especially grateful to Marcia Tanner for going out on this particular limb with me, and to Elizabeth Shepherd and Henry Hopkins at the UCLA Wight Art Gallery for deciding to keep such bad company.

Cheryl Dunye, the video curator for the programs shown in both East and West Coast exhibitions, has been wonderful to work with. Belonging to a younger generation, she has brought a fresh perspective to my own, and given me hope that women will continue to tear away at the obstructions to social equity.

Linda Goode Bryant, founder and director of *Just Above Midtown* from 1974 until its closing in 1986, has been a central force in bringing the work of artists of color to public attention. Throughout our long friendship, she has shared the evolution of her thoughts on the issues she addresses in her essay, which have greatly helped to clarify my own thinking.

The Henry Luce Foundation has provided major funding for this exhibition, which has been critical to the success of the project. Substantial support was also provided by Penny McCall, one of the original "bad girls," who has underwritten the costs of the catalogue. Many thanks for additional funding from the New York State Council on the Arts and The Director's Council of The New Museum, whose commitment to the Museum and to this exhibition in particular have made an enormous difference.

Susan Evans and Brian Sisco of Sisco & Evans Design, have that rare combination of sensitivity and adventurousness that have made working with them on the catalogue and related print materials a real pleasure. At the Museum, my colleagues Susan Cahan, Charlayne Haynes, France Morin and Laura Trippi read my essay and made many helpful comments and suggestions. Other friends and colleagues, particularly Eugene Metcalf, Leslie Satin, Margaret Curtis, Katie Clifford and Daniell Cornell, alerted me to source material I would otherwise not have been aware of. I'm especially grateful to Tim Yohn, who has edited all four catalogue manuscripts with care and thoughtfulness; over the years, his skill has shaped my own writing immeasurably and helped me to become better at it.

The "Zine," which started as a mental itch that said, "Why not try something a little different this time?" ended up being a 24-page takeoff on a 1950s pulp rag, thanks to the inventiveness of Emily Clark, Joan McClung and Marianne Morea, the design team at Neuberger and Berman that took on this job, *pro bono*, during their busiest season. And were it not for Arthur Goldberg's willingness to go for broke, so to speak, we wouldn't have been able to produce it at all.

The New Museum's Project Team for this exhibition has been invaluable in providing critical commentary which helped in the selection of specific works as well as to shape the project as a whole. I have them to thank for particularly lively and challenging discussions and support throughout. At the Museum, I've been lucky to work with colleagues who know a great deal more than I do about a wide variety of things. John Hatfield, our Registrar, and William Visnich, Installation Coordinator, are not only skilled, but have the patience of saints, as do our terrific crew members, artists all. Evan Kingsley very graciously and resourcefully covered for me under all kinds of circumstances and gave me the time to get the job done; a special thanks to Patricia Jones, whose talent and writing ability turned out the grants that got the support that got the show that included the artists who did the work.... My assistant Clare Micuda was adept at holding down the fort during an especially busy time and keeping everything running smoothly, for which I'm deeply grateful, and Aleya Saad was indispensible in organizing the opening events. And thanks to Suzy Spence for working on the *Bad Girls* products (Cups? T-Shirts? Who would've thought?), and to Amy Chen for helping immeasurably with the complicated administration and allocation of project funds. Mimi Young, Exhibition Coordinator, focused the entire project and kept us all on track, taming the many wild and erratic strands that make up an exhibition into a workable whole. Thank you, everyone, for making it possible for me to organize this exhibition, an activity usually forbidden to Museum directors!

Many people have pitched in to make things work, but I'm especially grateful to Greg Drasler, who was inexhaustible in pursuit of the images in the catalogue; to Willard Holmes, who came in to help tie loose ends together (literally and figuratively!) and who gave me invaluable feedback on my essay; to Gail Gregg, who has been enormously helpful in her intelligent responses to the ideas at the heart of the exhibition; to Dara Myers-Kingsley and Fran Seegull for early and inspired contributions; to Roz Warren, author of *Women's Glib* and many other wonderfully funny books, for her help in obtaining materials for the Reading Room; and to Nancy Dwyer, whose friendship and many contributions to the exhibition (including the logo) have helped me in innumerable ways. (And thank you, Dean, for all the talk, editing, support, dinners, cups of coffee, and for helping me to keep my own sense of humor intact.)

The Museum has a terrific internship program run by Jerry Philogene, but I have been especially fortunate in having four "interns" who have really been coordinators for the project and without whom it couldn't have happened. Brigitte Kölle, a young curator from Germany, worked with me on a daily basis for months, visiting studios, setting up tracking systems, providing research materials, helping indispensably to shape the exhibition as it developed. Sabine Ondraczek, who as it turned out comes from the same town as Brigitte, although they hadn't met previously, took up where she left off, providing assistance with every aspect of the show and sharing ideas until she returned to Germany in September, I daresay completely exhausted. I miss them both very much. Daniell Cornell, a doctoral candidate in art history at the Graduate Center of the City University of New York, began work on the project in September and has been an enormous help with virtually everything ever since; he also organized the bibliography and compiled the list of related exhibitions with skill and diligence, not to mention good cheer and considerable eyestrain. Melissa Goldstein, a talented artist I met in Seattle, decided to come to New York to work on the exhibition instead of exercising her many other options. She is absolutely central to this project: she has been a lifesaver, a delight, a diplomat, a juggler and a godsend; I cannot imagine how it could have been accomplished without her. I am not only grateful for the enormous amount of work these gifted and dedicated people did, but for their friendship, which has indelibly and joyfully marked this project.

The scope of the New York exhibition has been greatly enhanced by the collaboration of Michael Dorf of The Knitting Factory, who has programmed Wednesday night performances of bad girl music to coincide with the exhibition, and of Jonas Mekas of Anthology Film Archives, who has organized a series of bad girl films, which will run throughout Part II of our show.

And last but hardly least, thanks to the lenders to the exhibition for parting with their works and sending them into a world unknown, to the galleries for facilitating them (and much, much more), and to the participating artists, who have made working on it more than just pleasurable, but challenging and fun as well. I am especially grateful to the many artists who are *not* represented in the exhibition but whose efforts and ideas have informed it and whose work has helped to make the art world a place where women are seen and heard from in substantive and lasting ways.

Preface and Acknowledgments

Marcia Tanner

This Bad Girls thing started innocently. Marcia Tucker and I were talking about a phenomenon we'd both noticed: a spate of new work by artists, most of them women, which insouciantly tweaks the private parts of sacred bovines of all spots. Although concerned with sex and gender representations, the work has a distinctly different spirit from much of the "feminist" art of the 1970s and 80s. It's irreverent, anti-ideological, non-doctrinaire, non-didactic, unpolemical and thoroughly unladylike. Nothing is sacred to these artists. They take as axiomatic that all artists are natural-born outlaws, combine that with postmodernist theories that women (to quote critic Eileen Myles) are "inherently excessive and outside the law," and play with the consequences. Everything is up for grabs, especially the rule that serious art can't be funny.

Their art is seriously funny. The questions it raises are as complex as ever and possibly even more radical and outrageous than its predecessors', informed as it is by two decades of critical thinking and artmaking by feminists, gays and lesbians, and people of color. But the art looks seductive and inviting, disarmingly humorous and as sensuously beguiling as a cake with a dagger baked inside. It has a freedom and playfulness that's both evidence of liberation and enormously liberating itself.

The work was such a breath of iconoclastic fresh air that we two Marcias were exhilarated. It was like the call of the wild to our own inner (and outer) bad girls. Marcia Tucker told me she planned to organize a small exhibition called "Bad Girls" at The New Museum to document some of it. "Why don't you try to find a West Coast venue for a sister exhibition to run simultaneously?" she suggested.

I'd grown up in Hollywood and absorbed Judy Garland's and Mickey Rooney's "let's put on a show!" naivete. "Sure," I said, "Why not?" I was thinking: small alternative artists' space in San Francisco (where I live) and twelve, maybe thirteen artists.

Months later, having exhausted possibilities in the Bay Area, I wrote to Henry Hopkins, Director of UCLA's Wight Art Gallery, who had been my boss when he was director of the San Francisco Museum of Modern Art. This was a last resort, an act of desperation. I was certain no museum in a state-supported institution of higher education would have the guts to mount the show I had in mind.

Wrong. Elizabeth Shepherd, the Wight's curator, turned out to be a closet bad girl herself. She loved the idea and thought it should be a major exhibition. Meanwhile, Marcia Tucker was discovering so much strong new work in this vein that her modest original concept was also expanding. Suddenly bad girls were big.

Finding a venue for *Bad Girls West* in Los Angeles, in the very groin of Hollywood's male-dominated entertainment industry, was a terrific stroke of luck. It was a double homecoming, for me and for the work: the kind you dream about, combining fantasies of success and revenge. My mother brought me from Brooklyn to Hollywood when I was three to turn me into the next Shirley Temple/Margaret O'Brien. Not everyone takes celluloid or videotape so much to heart, but whether your gender ideals derive from *Casablanca* or *Wayne's World*, no one growing up in the U.S.A. escapes the influence of Hollywood's weirdly schizoid, overblown visions of how to act and look male or female in our culture. According to biographer Richard Reeves, even John F. Kennedy's sisters embraced Katherine Hepburn as their adolescent role model, watching her films over and over again to internalize her diction, mannerisms, style, the whole Hepburn gestalt.

Much of the work in both these exhibitions tackles and mischievously overturns aspects of sex and gender as perceived and purveyed by Hollywood: body- and self-image; sexuality and eroticism; gender roles, relationships and behavior; fashion, makeup and consumerism; celebrity, glamor, and aging; our very notions of "good girls" versus "bad girls" and how to tell the difference. Presenting this exuberant, subversive work in all its richness and variety will, we hope, add new dimensions to our understanding of the ways that culture shapes our notions of gender and thus the ways we see ourselves and others. And viewing it in the contexts of New York and Los Angeles, twin centers of the global image-manufacturing industry, should elaborate the work's meanings and make it even funnier and more pleasurable.

To organize such a complex exhibition and contribute to its accompanying catalogue have been both a rewarding personal odyssey and a richly collaborative undertaking, thanks to the support, encouragement, enthusiasm and collegial participation of a number of remarkable people. The project never would have happened in the first place without Marcia Tucker's inspiration and prescient nudging. Her inexhaustible generosity with introductions, contacts, suggestions, guidance and dialogue and her collaborative spirit have been utterly invaluable, as have her wisdom, experience, good sense, blessedly wicked sense of humor and, above all, her friendship. I really can't thank her enough.

From the project's inception, I've benefited from the cooperation, expertise and resources of many members of The New Museum's staff and internship program. Brigitte Kölle provided indispensable help with research, slides and logistics early on. A meeting with The New Museum's Bad Girls Project Team expanded and refined my thinking about *Bad Girls West*. Daniell Cornell made working on the Zine (our joint exhibition brochure) both fun and instructive, and Tim Yohn's careful, sympathetic editing of my catalogue essay made the editorial process less like a visit to the dentist than usual. Special thanks are due to Melissa Goldstein, who diligently and painstakingly marshalled and deployed a million details and communiques between New York and California to make both Zine and catalogue possible while somehow managing to maintain high spirits under tremendous pressure.

At the Wight Art Gallery, Henry Hopkins has my heartfelt thanks for his willingness to take a chance on a potentially controversial exhibition. I am truly grateful for his openness to the concept and for his moral support throughout the project's development. Elizabeth Shepherd lived up to and beyond her name. Not only has she been a wonderfully generous colleague, she gently yet firmly led me past many hazards into green pastures, and her tact, flexibility, unflagging enthusiasm and astringent sense of humor frequently restored my soul.

Other members of the Wight Art Gallery staff contributed significantly to the exhibition. If anybody could redeem the bad rap good girls get, it would be Farida Sunada, assistant to Elizabeth Shepherd. Combining superb organizational skills with efficiency, a diligent and meticulous eye for detail and a genuinely upbeat, uncloying optimism, she made the difficult look easy. I would especially like to thank her for her dedication and help in coordinating countless details of correspondence, travel arrangements, loan agreements, slide duplications and documentation.

Also at the Wight, Patricia Capps supplied expertise on administration and budgeting; Natalie Jacob assisted with the *Bad Girls* communications network connecting L.A. with the Bay Area and New York. Susan Lockhart managed the complex arrangements for shipping from private collections, museums and galleries around the country. Milt Young, assisted by Dave Paley and Will Reigle, handled the installation with creativity and great technical skill.

I deeply appreciate the generosity and enthusiastic participation of the private collectors who agreed to share their works with the public for *Bad Girls West*, and am grateful to the galleries, museums and their staffs for their help in securing loans and making work available.

While I'm responsible for *Bad Girls West* in its final form, many conversations and contacts with other curators and scholars helped steer me to artists and formulate my ideas. Karen Tsujimoto, curator of art at the Oakland Museum, gave me a tremendous boost early on by supplying me with her list of potential "bad girls" candidates; several participants in *Bad Girls West* were on her original roster. I'm very grateful to her and to the many others who generously shared their ideas and suggestions with me, including Kenneth Baker, Elizabeth Browne, Whitney Chadwick, Wanda Corn, Katherine Crum, Nancy Doll, Diana du Pont, Noriko Gamblin, Constance Lewallen, Dean McNeil, Stacey Moss, Sandra Phillips, Robert Riley, Fran Seegull, Marilyn Sode Smith, Terrie Sultan, and Jon Winet.

Of the many gratuitous acts of generosity and kindness that helped me as exhibition curator and essayist, the loan of a rare out-of-print edition of a book by Yoko Ono from Adrienne Fish of 871 Fine Arts in San Francisco stands out. On the private front, I doubt I could have made it without my own personal support system. Its main pillars are June Singer, the post-Jungian therapist, scholar and author I'm fortunate to have as my surrogate "laughing mother"; and my domestic partner Karl Sonkin, who does everything else, and extremely well too.

Bad Girls West was funded in part by the UCLA Art Council, the UCLA School of the Arts, and the California Arts Council. I am very grateful for their commitment and support.

Finally, I would like to thank from the bottom of my heart all the bad girls, actual and honorary, who really made this exhibition happen. I mean, of course, the participating artists. Working with them, sharing their ideas, creativity and humor, has been a privilege, an education, and a joy. I'm eager for the sequel.

The Attack of the Giant Ninja Mutant Barbies

Marcia Tucker

A Slice of Life

Nothing has captured the attention of the American public quite the way the recent case of a Virginia couple, Lorena and John Wayne Bobbitt, has. On June 23, 1993, while her husband was sleeping, the diminutive Mrs. Bobbitt, a 24-year-old manicurist, took a kitchen knife and separated John Wayne from his penis, later throwing it from the window of the car in which she fled. She claimed that she was distraught after he had choked and raped her for the second time in five days, and she wanted to put an end to years of repeated physical and sexual abuse.

While there has been a great show of support for Lorena Bobbitt, especially by women who feel that for once the punishment perfectly fits the crime, the "incident" has created a *frisson* of dread in many men. Several have had a more extreme reaction, like Marty Johns, a 31-year-old engineer who declared: "She ought to be executed."[1]

My guess is that Lorena Bobbitt was a good girl all her life—a traditional woman struggling to cope by repressing her rage and resentment; if she hadn't been she never would have put up with John Wayne. The furor and controversy (not to mention the jokes) engendered by her act and by her husband's acquittal on charges of rape and abuse indicate that despite the most recent quarter-century of effort by feminists working in women's studies, literary and psychoanalytic theory, the natural and behavioral sciences, and out on the streets, the dynamics of the bedroom, the office, or the factory haven't changed all that much for women. We're expected to be good girls, and that's that.

**Janna (owner of the Nail Sculptor salon where Lorena Bobbit works)
to Lorena: "Is that a penis in your pocket or are you just glad
to be out of the house?"**

A Hasty Hystery

Women who called themselves feminists in the late 1960s and early 1970s—
mostly young, white, middle class, formally educated, and heterosexual—
remember all too well the rigors of exploring the new territory called
Women's Liberation. From the early consciousness-raising sessions which
personalized vast inequities in status, behavior, opportunity, health care and
compensation between men and women, to the political and legislative work
which has only just begun to redress them, the Unwelcome Wagon of
Feminism has rolled relentlessly across America's fruited plains, picking up
passengers from the fields of critical theory, psychoanalysis, film and literary
studies, only to arrive at a place that, alas, looks a lot like the one we left, and
where they're still not happy to see us.

We rejected our parents "unliberated" behavior and their old-fashioned ideas
about the role of women and tried to find new ways to define ourselves. We
negotiated tortuous routes through debates about biology as destiny *("Sugar
and spice and everything nice/that's what little girls are made of")*, the social
construction of gender *("Sit up straight and behave yourself, Miss
Smartypants!")*, economic parity *("It's as easy to fall in love with a rich man as
a poor one")*, the authority of the phallocentric order *("Just you wait till your
father gets home!")*, childcare *("Don't just sit in the house all day, go outside and
play")*, the body *("I don't care if you don't like it, you'll eat it anyway")*, class
structure *("I'm not the maid in this house")*, race issues *("But some of my best
friends are....")* and the split between theory and practice *("You can't tell a
book by its cover")*, only to find that the world still seems uneasily divided
between "us" and "them," a division painfully concretized in the image of
Lorena Bobbitt racing from her bedroom, John Wayne's severed member in
her hand.

The divisions which characterized the early years of the Woman's Movement have become even more complex today, multiplying with the energy and persistence of fruit flies despite our increased awareness of them. It's not simply a gap in understanding between women and men, but between rich and poor, "white" and "non-white," straight and gay, butch and femme, Freudian and Lacanian, liberal and radical, nature and culture, parent and child, parent and childless. *Bad Girls* is an attempt to bridge these and other great divides, not by papering over them, but by finding a place where we can all talk.

The question is, who gets to do the talking?

Speak for Yourself

Women have fought for the right to speak and to be silent, to listen and to be heard, from the beginnings of the Suffrage movement before the turn of the century. The battle has become increasingly complex as the multiple, intricate and shifting nature of language itself has come to be understood.

Language is more than just what is spoken and written; virtually all communication, social structures and systems rely in some way on language for their form. Whoever controls language—who speaks, who is listened to or heard—has everything to say about how people think and feel about themselves. Language *is* power,

> even in the forms of the one-upsmanships of cocktail parties and the verbal muggings and discursive violences of everyday life. Power is exercised in the right to speak, the right to interrupt, the right to remain silent. Politics and language intersect in the form of attitudes, of talking down to or looking up to, of patronizing, respecting, ignoring, supporting, misinterpreting.[2]

When it comes to thinking about the different ways that women and men have been engaged with language, writer Teresa Bloomingdale provides a wicked indictment: "If you want to please your mother, talk to her. If you want to make points with your father, listen to him."[3]

When women *have* spoken and been heard, it has tended to be to and by each other, to women of the same race and class, and in forms which have been consistently ignored or undervalued by others. Thought of as singularly

Kathe Burkhart
Sayonara Cinderella, 1980

female, the uninscribed language of the anecdote, story, oral history, testimonial, slave and immigrant narrative, chant, ballad or song—as well as the more "trivial" forms of women's poetry, verse, autobiography, diary entries, personal correspondence and such—haven't been of much interest until very recently, and have had virtually no market beyond a small number of specialists. Works which do have a mass market among women, however—like soap operas, romance novels and certain kinds of movies—remain completely denigrated by everyone except those who admit to enjoying them. (Is it possible to be a feminist and a publicly declared "Dynasty" addict?)

In the visual arts, the process of "finding a voice" extending beyond the woman-to-woman domestic sphere has manifested itself in influential work by artists like Nancy Spero, Faith Ringgold, Mary Kelly, Adrian Piper, Jenny Holzer, Barbara Kruger and many others who use written text in their work to talk about such subjects as aging, racism, reproductive rights, motherhood, physical and sexual abuse, standards of beauty, and control of language itself. Spero's scrolls of mythical and legendary characters and text, Ringgold's story quilts, Kelly's first-hand accounts of women's views on aging, Piper's direct verbal/written instructions and questions to viewers about their racism, Jenny Holzer's invented slogans and truisms, and Kruger's "ads" all comprise a way of "talking" that is direct and uncompromising, and to which both lay and professional audiences can relate.

Language in the hands of the artists exhibited in *Bad Girls* differs from that of their predecessors and peers in its deliberately raucous humor; bad girls play with words by transforming them into objects, by rewriting narratives so that they conform to their own visions of the world, or by pointing to the absurd gulf between words and actions. (*"Do as I say, not as I do!"*) There is an endless flow of words in this exhibition, spilling and spewing, exhorting, insulting, cajoling, cheering and cursing.

Like the authors of feminist utopian novels that proliferated throughout the 1970s when the Women's Movement in the United States was gathering momentum, bad girl artists use language to disrupt stereotypes. These authors, who revolutionized the sci-fi genre, among others, also invented new terms and eliminated old ones in an attempt to reconfigure inherently sexist language. Terms like "fems" and "unmen" in Suzy McKee Charnas's *Motherlines* (1978), whose protagonist is distinguished from others of her kind by her ability to speak, were coined to define, enlarge on, and critique existing stereotypes. Literature, performance and the visual arts have all pro-

vided different kinds of speculative narratives as a way both to criticize a world seen as created by and for men and to project non-hierarchic alternatives to it.[4] Bad girls bring laughter to this language, using it to talk about what is wrong, what can continue to go wrong or get worse, and what can be be envisioned as better in a gender-divisive world.

Those who have been denied a voice, especially by being ignored outside the domestic sphere to which they have been consigned, tend to get pretty angry when they realize what's happened. When the women of my mother's generation said to their children, "I'm not asking you, I'm telling you," they meant business, because it was the only kind of business they weren't kept out of. The anger that occurs when one is being spoken *for* is even worse. As Mae Gwendolyn Henderson puts it in discussing the situation for black women, "the development from voicelessness to voice, from silence to tongues...does not exist without intervention by the other(s) who speak for and about [her.] In other words, it is not that black women, in the past, have had nothing to say, but rather that they have had no say."[5]

Making the task of speaking increasingly difficult on all fronts is the frightening rise of right-wing fundamentalism, which has attempted to silence dissident artistic voices in various unsubtle ways ranging from death threats to the rescinding of public funding. Gay and lesbian voices particularly, as well as those of male and female artists of color and women who assert their sexuality from a woman's perspective have become the most pointed targets of attack.

And alas, the censorship vendetta has recently gained reenforcements through the efforts of "anti-porn" feminists who object to the role they feel all pornography plays in promoting violence against women. Because the distinctions between pornography and, for example, erotica made by women for women, sexually explicit works of art, or pornographic images used by feminist artists as critique are blurred in this blanket condemnation, such censorship has the potential to close down an exhibition of work by a photographer like Sally Mann as well as the 42nd Street "peep" shows. Thus, feminist is busy silencing feminist, leaving the field to the Moral Majority who are all too happy to appropriate feminist language as new ammunition for their own smoking guns.

These distinctions notwithstanding, as Tania Modleski says, "for women, who throughout most of history have not been given political representation or a political voice—a state of affairs that has made them the *true* silent majority—there is little reason to be sanguine about the possibilities of a revolution based on the mute tactics of the eternal 'feminine.'"[6]

Uh-oh. Sounds like a job for the Bad Girls!!! Bad girls aren't polite, they're aggressive. They speak before (and while) they're spoken to. They interrupt. What's more, they *prefer* to talk with their mouths full. They use language that's vulgar or downright obscene, and don't stop when their mothers threaten to wash their mouths out with soap. They curse, rant and rave, and make fun of and mimic whomever and whatever they want, themselves included.

"One great thing to do ... is to get out one of your tampons and just put it behind your ear. It is a riot! Put it behind your ear, and just walk around. Walk around. And then when somebody comes up to you and says, 'Uh, you've got a tampon behind your ear,' then you say, 'Oh my God, where *is* my pencil?'"

—Kate Clinton quoted in "Women's Comic Visions."

The reason for all this talk about talking is that talk is hardly cheap, popular belief notwithstanding. All we need to do is to think about all the women who've been told to shut up because they were making waves: Betty Friedan, Joan Rivers, Jane Fonda, Angela Davis, Anita Hill, NEA *refusées* Holly Hunter and Karen Finley, and scores of others, all following in the courageous and stubborn wake of Joan of Arc (who, as we know, was burned at the stake in a last attempt to get her to keep her mouth shut). Power—the power to name oneself, to be a speaking subject rather than the silent object of someone else's ideas, formulations or images—means agency. And clearly, the restoration of subjectivity, voice and agency to those who have not had it is a crucial project of feminism.

17 year old Amy Fisher, serving a 5 to 15 year sentence for shooting Mary Jo Buttafuoco last year, testified: "Joseph Buttafuoco has publicly labeled me as crazy, psychopathic, depraved and unworthy of belief... an obsessed teenager fantasizing a relationship with a married man who was faithful to his marriage and family... He entered a plea of guilty because he is, in fact, guilty... I can accurately describe unique physical markings which only a person who had been intimate with him would know." Mr. Buttafuoco was sentenced to six months for statutory rape, admitting: "Sometimes lust takes me over. It's very painful." His wife Mary Jo maintains, "I choose to believe, based on the person that I know and the person that I live with...and the person whose bed I share, that he did not have an affair with her."

—from *The New York Post* and *The Daily News,* November 16, 1993

Step right up, Ladies and Gentlemen....

Two events last fall helped to focus my thinking about *Bad Girls*. One was a spontaneous visit to Coney Island, much diminished since its heyday, but nonetheless still exuding an aura of freedom and excitement; the other was my annual participation, with friends and family, in the Greenwich Village Halloween Parade.

When I was a child, Coney Island was a fairground, circus, parade, and out-door eatery rolled into one; even parents gave up their last vestiges of dignity in the thrall of the Carousel (mostly Moms) or the Parachute Ride (mostly Dads). In the postwar 1940s, the amusement park and boardwalk still fea-tured sideshows advertising exotic dancers, freaks and wonders (the latter mostly consisting of mutant fetuses crammed into jars of formaldehyde) which were forbidden to children by parents and law, but clandestinely visited all the same by misbehaving boys and bad girls.

Perhaps the closest thing to the original Coney Island in New York today is the downtown Halloween Parade, where misbehaving has been raised to a high art form. Some of the traditionally sanctioned trappings of the formal parade can be found here—marching bands and drum majorettes, for instance, albeit in drag, and as at the Macy's Thanksgiving Day parade there are floats, but they are homemade and wildly fanciful. This parade's participants, however, are as diverse as the city's population and as unconventional as everyone assumes its downtown denizens to be. You don't need a permit to march—you just get in line at the staging area. It's a people's parade, growing bigger and more popular every year, the sidewalks on Sixth Avenue from Spring Street to 23rd Street packed deep with cheering, costumed spectators. Even an occasional cop on duty sports vampire teeth. At the end, the marchers wind back downtown along the sidewalks in search of a late supper, continuing their revelry with strangers and friends well into the night.

Thinking about the ways in which the carnival atmosphere of Halloween gives celebrants license to look and act differently, to be out of control, to be frightened or frightening without consequences, to find comfort in the company of strangers and to experience solidarity with crowds, led me to think about *Bad Girls* in terms of the carnivalesque.

There has been a growing interest in recent years among contemporary cultural critics and theorists in the nature of carnival as a key to understanding human behavior. Described by critics Peter Stallybrass and Allon White as "a loose amalgam of procession, feasting, competition, games and spectacle," and "the repeated, periodic celebration of the grotesque body—fattening food, intoxicating drink, sexual promiscuity, altered ego-identity, the inverse and the heteroglot,"[7] carnival activity has striking parallels to the bad girls sensibility.

I have drawn extensively on writings by and about the Russian author and theorist Mikhail Bakhtin (1895-1975), whose early work was suppressed by Stalinist purges of the 1930s and which only relatively recently became available in English. Bakhtin has been influential for developing theories of the carnivalesque in literature that are applicable to many realms of culture. These ideas are closely allied to his formulation of the shifting, multiple, interactive and socially determined nature of language, which he called "dialogical"—a formulation that stemmed in part from a distaste for what he perceived as the presumption of a singular, authoritative voice in literary and interpretive texts, a voice that does not take into consideration the relational nature of language nor the presence of a social context in which language always takes place.[8]

The basic concepts of carnival can provide a framework for the understanding of recent works of art about feminist and gender issues, particularly those which are trying to effect positive social change by being both transgressive and funny (hoping to kill more flies with honey than with the fly-swatter).[9] Pervasive and liberating laughter is indigenous to carnival, as is its democratic nature. It is characterized by an inordinate ability to mix disparate elements with wild abandon and to confound categories, social positions and hierarchies of space, language and class; to provide both a "festive critique" and an extreme utopian vision of society at the same time; and to reconfigure the world through laughter.[10] Carnival was a social space where suppressed appetites could be expressed and sated, where inversions of power and position were temporarily sanctioned, where sexual dimensions could be explored without reprisal. In short, it was an arena where pleasure reigned.

When Mikhail Bakhtin writes about carnival he is talking not about its modern manifestations and appropriations, but about the kind of pre-Lenten festivities which had roots in pre-Christian Greece and Rome, reached an epic intensity in the Middle Ages, and continued through to the mid-nineteenth century. Some aspects of carnival culture survive today, most notably in the Mardi Gras of New Orleans (stemming from a European cultural tradition) and in the carnivals of Brazil and the West Indies (with roots as well in the rituals and celebrations of various African spiritual and social practices).

Unlike a visit to Coney Island, Atlantic City, the circus, or Disneyland today, carnival wasn't simply a matter of a vacation or a break from one's normal daily grind. The effect of the carnivalesque was no less than a revolution, no matter how transitory. The forms that carnival has taken today are different in both shape and content, intention and effect, from those of the Middle Ages, because the increasing suppression of carnival from the seventeenth century on by the rising bourgeoisie has virtually eliminated all but its most institutionalized, ritualized and commercial forms. Contemporary forms of carnival are designed to appease people by giving them permission to let off steam, thus preventing any real political ferment. And other appetites unleashed in carnival have come to be satiated through rampant consumerism, so that the genuine symbolic inversion of carnival cross-dressing, for example, has today been coopted as a harmless fashion statement, promoted by the industry for its own purposes. Antisocial behaviors, it seems, can be appropriated for consumerist ends with very little opposition. (See, for example, the recent Calvin Klein underwear ads starring rap singer Marky Mark.) The real subversiveness and the pointed humor of the work in *Bad*

Girls aren't easily commodifiable, but the term and its connotations have already become institutionalized in a variety of forms. The widespread popularity of the black leather motorcyle jackets worn by everyone, from five-year-old girls to matinee matrons and society patrons, hardly constitutes a revolutionary political act. It will take a real challenge to the *places* that institutionalize transgression (including museums!) to effect any genuine transformation. But in terms of artmaking and the politics of the art world, bad girls have taken an aggressive role in posing such challenges.[11]

In the hands of these artists, carnival attributes, particularly the emancipating force of laughter, have nonetheless accomplished a refreshing change of perspective. As Robert Stam describes it, carnival

> abolishes hierarchies, levels social classes, and creates another life free from conventional rules and restrictions. In carnival, all that is marginalized and excluded—the mad, the scandalous, the aleatory—takes over the center in a liberating explosion of otherness. The principle of material body—hunger, thirst, defecation, copulation—becomes a positively corrosive force, and festive laughter enjoys a symbolic victory over death, over all that is held sacred, over all that oppresses and restricts.[12]

Perhaps most important of all is that the observer of carnival festivities is also a participant, even if intermittently, and so the relationship between observer and "performer" is one of exchange and dialogue.[13] Turning observers into participants creates a sense of community among carnival's very diverse constituents. Such, too, is the democratic and popular nature of the humor integral to *Bad Girls.* Humor is an exercise in mutual experience and empathy; when you laugh, it means that you've understood or "gotten" the joke, that you've been able to see a new set of relationships in a given situation. It also, of course, helps if you're not the one who is being made fun of.

The central activity of the carnival, itself a kind of giant playground, is playing, which Susan Suleiman describes as "fantasy,. as free invention, as mastery, as mockery, as parody [and] as transgression,"[14] all key elements not only in the avant-garde Surrealist aesthetic, but in the early modernist aesthetic that has provided a broad base (*not* a pedestal) for bad girl artistic enterprise.[15] (It was usually those boys who had to be pushed out of the house to play and those girls who never stayed indoors playing house who ended up in the arts, so perhaps all this comes as no surprise.)

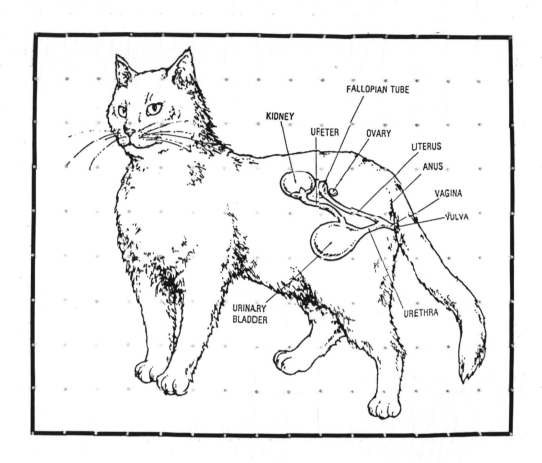

Judith Weinperson
Read My Pussy, 1992

Providing the strongest opposition to the flexibility and openness of play are the Moral Majority and the religious fundamentalists, who insist on single, one-dimensional interpretations of all texts and images, whether they like them or not. Their blanket condemnation of works containing sexual imagery of any kind makes me think of the general public's similar reading of nonobjective or conceptual works of art, not to mention feminism, which the media and a large part of the public have tried to flatten into the image of a manic group of bra-burning, man-hating, frustrated women.[16]

"It may have escaped your notice that recently a vacuum cleaner just like this one and the one down in your basement was sold for $100,000. Also a sink went for $121,000, and a pair of urinals for $140,000. All of the above and even more unlikely stuff is art. That's what the artists say, the dealers and of course the people who lay out good money. It all may make you believe in the wisdom of P.T. Barnum that there is a sucker born every day, but it is what the art world has become...."

—Morley Safer, on "60 Minutes," September 19, 1993

The particular form of play called parody, which for Bakhtin was "the privileged mode of artistic carnivalization,"[17] has been a familiar dish at the cultural table for centuries, albeit still an acquired taste among the *haute bourgeoisie.* This is because parody uses the master's tools to trash the master's house while (at least in the hands of bad girls) building on a new wing for the mistress. Parody also finds a home today in hip-hop culture and some rap music, where it functions as a survival tactic, a way of dismantling the house without having to go to jail for it. In such popular television shows as "In Living Color" or the somewhat less risky "Saturday Night Live," we can see comedy's liberating effect as it turns language around in order to actively create rather than passively reflect reality; as the advertisement for "Comic Justice," a black program on The Comedy Channel states, it's "the only weapon we have left."[18]

Bad girls have been using parody to poke fun at work that is more likely to get shown, written about, funded and bought because, all else being equal, the artist has a penis rather than a vagina. The past few years have seen a proliferation of work by women which appropriates the signature styles of "big-time"

Jacqueline Hayden
Figure Model Series, 1992

male artists and makes slight alterations to turn those styles against themselves, into feminist critiques.[19] But irritation is more likely to prompt parody than rage, which tends to destroy the model rather than simply alter it.

Since parody remains tied to the form it mocks, many bad girls have turned from parody to a humorous deconstruction of social inequities as they are manifest in the larger arenas of marriage, fashion, religion, art history, childrearing, hierarchies of class and race, and the corporate world's "glass ceiling." It is this comic sensibility, I think, that distinguishes today's feminists, both those of a younger generation who have benefited from their mothers' rage as well as those mothers themselves who have survived it. (Here some of us are, out of the frying pan into the fire, facing a somewhat different but no less rigorous engagement with middle age, an engagement whose most useful tool is also—guess what?—a sense of humor.)

Because the avant-garde, with its fundamentally aggressive nature, has always been situated at the margins of artistic practice, where women are also most often found, their combined transgressive potential is enormous. (Imagine, if you will, a lesbian cross-dresser who pumps iron, looks like Chiquita Banana, thinks like Ruth Bader Ginsburg, talks like Dorothy Parker, has the courage of Anita Hill, the political acumen of Hillary Clinton, and is as pissed off as Valerie Solanas, and you really have something to worry about.)

Traditionally, the role of the avant-garde has been to turn things upside-down and to challenge official or sanctioned culture, a role linking it to carnival's symbolic inversion of everything in sight. In the mid- to late-sixteenth century, firsthand accounts of carnival processions mentioned transvestites and participants dressed as clergy, while popular visual representations of the period included such images as a servant riding with the king walking behind him, a general being inspected by a private, a wife beating her husband, or a child caring for an infantilized parent.[20] In carnival festivities, the lower classes aped the manners and pretensions of the aristocracy, making fun of those of higher status by "bringing them down to size," and at the same time reveling in their ability to do so. Literally and figuratively, the marginalized played with the powerful, a mouse holding the cat at bay.

A familiar kind of symbolic inversion is that of role reversal, a tool of a particular strand of feminist theory, as well as of women's stand-up comedy. Role reversal in what has come to be called "cultural feminism" takes qualities such as intuition, spirituality and nurturance to be uniquely female and superior,

leading to the establishment of a countercanon in which the formerly suppressed or neglected work of women writers, artists, musicians, and so on, can be recuperated and supported.[21] The key to social change in this version of feminism is the substitution of a supposedly kinder, gentler feminine ethos and praxis for an ignorant and oppressive masculine one. The idea that if men were responsible for the childrearing, domestic chores, cooking and coffee-klatches, the women would be free to run the world in a better way, for instance, continues to provide reams of great comic material.

Carnival activity is "symbolic action which is rarely mere play, [but rather] articulates cultural and political meanings."[22] But "mere" play is also a form of entertainment, so that the symbolic inversions of the powerful and the powerless, male and female, old and young, rich and poor, or "high" and "low" provide a pleasurable, relatively inexpensive tasting menu of potential social change.

> From *If Men Could Become Pregnant:* "There would be macho movies about childbirth. Clint Eastwood would clench his teeth, squint and say, 'Make my day,' while pushing; Sylvester Stallone would grunt and sweat profusely while going through a contraction. A movie called *Deliverance* would have a whole new meaning."
>
> —Mary Grabar, in *Women's Glib*

Cammi Toloui
The Pleasure Palace, 1993 (detail)

Talking out of both sides of your mouth

The populist, utopian vision of the carnival and fair is characterized by Bakhtin's dialogical voice, a voice which interrupts any singular narrative with one that runs counter to it, comments upon it, mocks or critiques it. The dialogical voice provides alternative and multiple points of view, aligning itself with open and fluid systems of exchange and circulation rather than with the singular, closed and static forms of the classical mode. A conversation rather than a monologue, in feminist comic work the dialogical voice can be a real exchange, à la Gracie Allen and George Burns, or the kind of internal dialogue used so brilliantly by Dorothy Parker in short stories like "The Waltz," with its droll contrast between inner and outer voices:

> *Ow!* For God's sake, don't *kick*, you idiot; this is only second down. Oh, my shin. My poor, poor shin, that I've had ever since I was a little girl! "*Oh, no, no, no. Goodness, no. It didn't hurt the least little bit. And anyway it was my fault. Really it was. Truly. Well, you're just being sweet, to say that. It really was all my fault.*" I wonder what I'd better do—kill him this instant, with my naked hands, or wait and let him drop in his traces....[23]

This split between public and private has ramifications for other kinds of dichotomies, like that of the "good" and "bad" mother, the former nurturing, the latter creative. Women have struggled to reconcile this "maternal splitting" for centuries in the face of societal contraints that hold the two to be mutually incompatible. Bad girls refuse this view of motherhood and insist on the continuity and compatibility of parenting *and* being part of the paid workforce. They also make fun of the sanctity of motherhood, playing with their children and themselves in ways which sometimes touch a raw nerve for those who uphold a singular view of "family values."

The dialogical voice is perfectly suited to the humorous and subversive tactics of bad girls, partly because it is impolite and aggressive, saying what cannot otherwise be articulated; making the private all too public is one of the humorist's greatest skills. In that sense, the dialogical voice is welcomed. But it's also the voice that tells the truth, that breaks taboos, and is most apt to be feared, "cured" or silenced. It's the voice of the ventriloquist's dummy, the uninhibited child, the court jester and the hysteric.

My Body Lies Over the Ocean...

Mikhail Bakhtin counters the still-pervasive eighteenth-century ideals of rationality with an alternative logic, a logic of excess, of the lower bodily stratum, of
the grotesque, which "could unsettle 'given' social positions and interrogate
the rules of inclusion, exclusion and domination which structured the social
ensemble."[24] Here, perhaps, is another crucial link between the features of
carnival and the work of vanguard artists worldwide in which an astonishing
proliferation of bodily images flirts with, if not openly celebrates, the
grotesque.[25]

**"[For the exhibition,] a basic structural idea was developed that attacks visitors,
seduces them, threatens, confuses, caresses, relaxes, so that art can be
rediscovered as an independent, different, alien force."**
—Press release by Jan Hoet, organizer of the 1992 *Documenta* in Kassel, Germany

The grotesque body is frightening to most people. It stands in opposition to
the ideal of the serene, closed, symmetrical and centered classical form sanctioned by high or official culture (particularly the fashion magazines).
Actually, the grotesque body could hardly be said to "stand," since it's more
apt to be all over the place, bulging, multiple, excessive, and constantly changing. But a further description is in order:

> It is an image of impure corporeal bulk with its orifices (mouth, flared
> nostrils, anus) yawning wide and its lower regions (belly, legs, feet,
> buttocks and genitals) given priority over its upper regions (head,
> "spirit," reason)...it is always in process, it is always becoming, it is a
> mobile and hybrid creature, disproportionate, exorbitant, outgrowing
> all limits, obscenely decentered and off-balance, a figural and symbolic
> resource for parodic exaggeration and inversion.[26]

The grotesque body, by virtue of its lack of stable boundaries, its ingestions
and excretions, its openings and orifices, breaks the confines between the body
and the world.[27] It is engaged and interactive. And it is indisputably female.

This transgressive figure contradicts commonly-held values and norms of all
kinds. It is old, pregnant, horny, loud, fat, sloppy and drunk, and it's telling
the authorities to get fucked. No wonder it's scary. And no wonder the ideal

female form in which all grotesque aspects are hidden from view (at least in mainstream Western culture), the one bad girls don't buy, is the one which is under the complete control of its owner and of its leasing corporation, The Fashion Industry.

> **"If a woman gets nervous, she'll eat or go shopping.**
> **A man will attack a country—it's a whole other way of thinking."**
>
> —Elayne Boosler, quoted in *In Stitches*.

Bad Girls has a field day with transgressive bodies. Not only do images of women who defy stereotypical media conventions proliferate, but they're images of women in their infinite variety, made with affection and exuberance, transgressive simply because they're so different from the ways we see women usually represented. *Bad Girls* puts the lie to stereotypical images of the female body by showing it unidealized and unselfconscious, a challenge to the inevitable accusation of inherent female narcissism; it makes it clear that what's normal depends on who's doing the defining, and from what position.

A contemporary manifestation of interest in the grotesque body is the public's fascination with "freaks," those human anomalies also euphemistically referred to as "strange people" (or simply "entertainers"). As Leslie Fiedler points out, "freaks" have captured the imaginations of "normal" people for centuries, providing them with an image of their secret fears in the literalized form of the extremes of human physiognomy.[28] Contemporary popular culture continues its fascination with the deformed and disfigured through plays and films like *Frankenstein, The Elephant Man, The Phantom of the Opera,* and *The Man with No Face.*

It is no accident that the term "freak" was also used to describe the drug users, dropouts and dissidents of the early 1960s, some of whom helped instigate not only the student uprisings of 1968, but the burgeoning Women's Liberation Movement that same year. Janis Joplin was the idol and role model of the period, giving voice to the plaints and longings of an entire generation, shaking blues, rock 'n roll and myriad black and white musical sources into her own seductive and ultimately lethal cocktail. Like Joplin, "freaks" hated authority, looked, dressed and acted differently from "normal" people, and were given to kinky sex with strangers and other out-of-body experiences; in short, they set a new standard for inventive antisocial behavior.

The term was appropriated in the early 1970s by underground cartoonists like Robert Crumb, Gilbert Shelton, Bill Griffiths, and even Art Spiegelman, whose mutant characters starred in a variety of misadventures. "Freaking out" as a result of drugs and modern life, these new heros and heroines were everything the 1950s feared and despised. At the same time, X-rated comics proliferated, among them *Home Grown Funnies, Zap Comics, Young Lust, Bijou Funnies, Big Ass, Uneeda Comix* (with Honeybunch, "who joins the Women's Movement and learns to kick ass") and *Motor City Comics* (starring Lenore Goldberg and her Girl Commandos). Although singularly lacking in the work of women cartoonists and often deeply misogynist in tone, they laid the groundwork for the bad girls comic book artists and cartoonists working today.

Child's Play

Contemporary analyses have pointed to the relationship of childhood rituals and games and carnivalesque practices.[29] As comedians like Lily Tomlin and the late Gilda Radner demonstrate, transforming oneself into a child literalizes the urge to play. In the early years of "Saturday Night Live," Gilda's hyperkinetic Brownie, Judy Miller, misbehaved hilariously, with no mediation between imagination and conduct. In the theater and on television specials, Lily's Edith Ann, seated in her giant chair, uncovered the lies and hypocrisies of the grownup world with mischievous guile. This is not the needy, whimpering, hurt, neglected "inner child" of new age psycho*dreck*, but a powerful, uncensored, transgressive force erupting from the body, telling the grownups to take a hike. This is the bad girls version of the evil brats in such films as *Village of the Damned, The Bad Seed,* and *The Good Son*, making you laugh while they scare you.

The transgressive body not only mutates from old to young and back, but across genders, redefining itself in multiple ways, rejecting any fixed form. Performance artists of all kinds have been defining their bodies for themselves in analogous ways. Some have been giving workshops which deal with gender bending, like those of Diane Torr (who teaches the basics of cross-dressing for both sexes, but on separate days) or with role playing, like Annie Sprinkle's ongoing lessons in how to become a "sex goddess" or "slut." Gender identity is also explored in the work of male performance artists like John Kelly, Hunter Reynolds and the late Ethyl Eichelberger, who trace a dual lineage in cross-dressing: one branch stems from Marcel Duchamp's famous alter ego,

Rrose Selavy; the other, more recent, comes from Divine (the protagonist of such outrageous John Waters films as *Pink Flamingoes* or *Hairspray*) and works its way through to the widely popular, straight "I can fool 'em *and* be a better woman than women can" antics of Dustin Hoffman in *Tootsie* or, more recently, Robin Williams as *Mrs. Doubtfire.*

At a panel discussion about the existence of a "homosexual esthetic" held in 1982, the writer Bertha Harris commented that "what America hates and fears above all is the 'bull dyke.'"[30] Her statement was greeted by a roar of appreciative laughter from the audience, because she had gone straight to the heart of the matter. If the lesbian body—even the *idea* of the lesbian body—is repugnant to a majority of the straight world (unless it's in *femme* form and engaged in sex for the enjoyment of male viewers), its most extreme embodiment, the "bull dyke," is the grotesque and transgressive body *par excellence.* This is because the female body above all is the instrument through which society's standards of propriety, appearance and behavior are expressed. A man who dresses outside the norm is considered an eccentric, a dandy or an absent-minded professor (whose wife, if he has one, is away visiting her mother), whereas for women "the seriousness with which we take questions of dress and appearance is betrayed by the way we regard *not* taking them seriously as an index of...serious psychological problems."[31] *("Just look at yourself...!")*

A woman who wrests control of her own body from the media's image of what she should look like, who has no interest in having her body crippled, mutilated, bound or surgically altered, or who does not even care to simply modify it to enhance her attractiveness to men, undermines society's standards and is therefore seen as politically dangerous rather than simply aesthetically dissident. The "bull dyke" is doubly powerful because she has taken on masculine attributes as well as fulfilling her own desires by redesigning her body for herself. Can you imagine the American public responding to a lesbian version of *Tootsie* or *Mrs. Doubtfire* with the same warmth and enthusiasm?

Attempts to suppress the lesbian body are reminiscent of nineteenth-century attempts to cure the hysterical body. Significantly, the woman's body was the battleground on which repression was played out in the form of hysteria, particularly the fear of what Freud, in *Studies on Hysteria,* termed those "agencies of disgust"—dirt, disease, and fat.[32] Hysterical behavior resembled carnival "madness," infused as it was with many of the same attributes—"eating, inversion, mess, dirt, sex and stylized body movements."[33] Certainly repressed and sublimated desires and terrors erupted into the extreme bodily antennuations and pantomimed gestures of the hysterical body, whose rigidly stylized postures referred to the impulses, pleasures, and excesses it was not free to indulge in.[34] Thus, the "mad" body was a vehicle for the expression of those impulses, no matter how distorted, while the "sane" body, bound by society's strictures, was not. (The term hysteria has, thankfully, all but disappeared as a designation of female pathology; it survives in this sense only in the popular adjectival form used by men to refer to women when they show emotion.)

The inherent theatricality of hysteria was demonstrated in the drama of neurologist Jean Martin Charcot's psychoanalytical "theater" of the late 1800s to which, strange as it may seem today, lay observers were welcomed, as they were to other kinds of "scientific" theaters of the period. Directed, choreographed and documented by Charcot, the staging of female hysteria was the nineteenth-century equivalent of a Broadway smash hit. As Elaine Showalter points out, Charcot not only believed that he was formulating and codifying the gestural laws of hysteria, but taught them to his patients, who then "performed" them for an almost exclusively masculine audience. Indeed, painted images of the gestures, like crib notes, were hung throughout Salpêtrière, the hospital where Charcot worked. Showalter notes that these "*attitudes passionelles*" were strikingly similar to the stylized movements of French theater and melodrama at that time, particularly to those of the musician and teacher François Delsarte, who also was developing a "scientific" system of gesture for the purpose of musical and dramatic expression.[35] Showalter, however, speculates that Charcot's concern with the frozen gesture of hysteria may in fact point more toward its relationship to photography and painting than to theater, the realm to which Freud's theories would seem to lead; in fact, many of the once-pleasurable images and symbols of European carnival discussed in *Studies on Hysteria* became transformed into the symptoms of hysteria.[36]

Charcot and Freud notwithstanding, theater was in fact one of the few places in the arts where women were allowed to work, perhaps because the theater was a space set apart from the activities of everyday life, and because acting was seen as interpretive rather than creative.[37] Women were integral to the history of burlesque theater in America, which took the country by storm in 1869 and died out only after the Depression. Burlesque was initially the domain of women writers, producers, and performers, who sang, danced, cross-dressed, and mocked the pretentiousness of high culture, the behavior

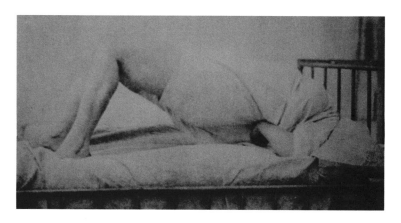

Photograph from Jean Martin Charcot, *Invention de l'hystéria: Charcot et l'iconographie Photographique de la Salpêtrière*, 1877-1880

of the predominantly male theatergoers and the antics of men in general. Originally, burlesque, like carnival, was subversive, outrageous, and wickedly funny. It also shared with the carnival a resistance to any unified theatrical form, remaining open, antiauthoritarian, and multivocal, with no claim to a single author or point of view. In his fascinating analysis of the genre, *Horrible Prettiness*, Robert Allen points out that the earliest burlesque pieces in America ended with references to female suffrage because the form emerged at a time of deep concern with gender definitions. In his words, "the burlesque is one of several nineteenth-century entertainment forms that is grounded in the aesthetics of transgression, inversion, and the grotesque,"[38] although it became increasingly debased and is today remembered only as a place where female bodies and female sexuality were on display (and often available for purchase).

"Acting" also had a function outside the theater as a survival technique for people duplicitously forced into behaving submissively while thinking subversively. It remains even today a skill learned readily by the oppressed, "who often appear to acquiesce in the oppressor's ideas about [them], thus producing a double meaning: the same language or act simultaneously confirms the oppressor's stereotypes of the oppressed and offers a dissenting and empowering view for those in the know."[39] But separate strands of the tangled skein of carnival, hysteria, and the theater have been taken up by bad girls working in all media, from the more traditional forms of painting and sculpture to performance art's relatively new interweavings of dance, theater, music, demonstration, tableaux and stand-up comedy.

"Mobs of scribbling women"

Until about 50 years ago, the theater was a democratic form of entertainment, relatively inexpensive and available to a wide variety of people. Today it has become, like the opera, a spectacle accessible only to the privileged. But bad girl performance artists, like their counterparts in the visual arts, have been engaged in scaling a Berlin Wall between the art world and popular culture. They follow in the wake of comedians like Whoopi Goldberg, Roseanne Arnold and Lily Tomlin, who in turn could not have scrambled over it without standing on the shoulders of the likes of Mabel Normand (the famous film comedian of the 1910s) or Moms Mabley (the great stand-up comic whose career spanned five decades, from the 1920s to her death in 1975). They, in turn, owe their successful climb in part to such early burlesque queens as Lydia Thompson and Pauline Markham, whose talent, looks and audacity appealed equally to bourgeois as well as to working-class audiences. The continued attempt to keep "high art" and "popular culture" apart, like Romeo and Juliet, seems doomed despite the best efforts of the Montagues and Capulets of culture to maintain the separation.

"You teach 'em Mother Hubbard went to the cupboard to get her poor dog a bone. I say Mother Hubbard had gin in that cupboard. You tell 'em Jack and Jill went up the hill after some water. I tell 'em water don't run uphill. You tell 'em Mary had a little lamb. I tell 'em wasn't the doctor surprised. Sure the cow jumped over the moon; you would have jumped too; that man's hand was cold! You tell 'em the wolf ate up Red Riding Hood's grandmother. I tell 'em if he did, then he must have used tenderizer. As tough as Grandmother was, that wolf had a hard time!"

—Moms Mabley, quoted in *Women's Comic Visions.*

Since the nineteenth century, "authentic" art has been configured as masculine, its priests and acolytes all too happy to be saved from the contaminating effects of the inferior, grossly sexual, kitschy blight of mass and popular culture, configured as feminine.[40] In Andreas Huyssen's analysis, the trajectory of modernism contains "a powerful masculinist and misogynist current...which time and again openly states its contempt for women and for the masses."[41] Fear of the uncontrollable, the irrational, the sexual, and the unconscious, seen as embodied in both women and the masses, means that both are held to pose a political threat to the social status quo.[42] Insofar as women have been held responsible for "the debasement of taste and the sentimentalisation of culture,"[43] and the masses have been held to have no taste or culture at all, both pose a threat to the aesthetic status quo as well.

As Huyssens points out, high art and mass culture have finally begun a reluctant dialogue partly as a result of feminist activity in the arts, and partly because of recent interest in the neglected forms of cultural expression which are being used increasingly by women, mainstream be damned. (Anyhow, as comedian Kate Clinton says, the mainstream is wide and shallow and slow-moving; it's the tributaries that are deep and fast, and where all the fun is.)

Race to the Finish

The real reason that its detractors consider mass or popular culture debased is not limited to the question of women: it is also associated with the working classes, as well as with the racial and ethnic "other." The neglected forms of cultural expression associated with both range from the musical to the literary; they include white working-class folk music (mining and railroad songs or camp-meeting gospel hymns, for instance); call-and-response singing and blues in black communities; or the life narratives of all kinds of people who work in the backyards, kitchens, laundry rooms, and nurseries of their wealthier employers (or husbands). These forms of artmaking, because they are so deeply embedded in lived experience, blur the lines between art and everyday life.

Like blacks, Jews in America and Europe had a long history of oppression and became expert at cultural mimicry and masquerade, although it has been easier to assimilate (or to "pass") because of their skin color, Hitler notwithstanding. Interestingly, Jewish entertainers like Al Jolson and Eddie Cantor took up blackface, which was a part of the established nineteenth-century theatrical tradition called minstrelsy, perhaps out of the peculiar combination of what Eric Lott identifies as "panic, anxiety, terror and pleasure" in response to black culture,[44] or perhaps, as Irving Howe suggests, as an expression of affinity, "with one woe speaking through the voice of another."[45]

The minstrel show was a form of entertainment for the white industrial labor force from the 1830s to the 1850s, wildly popular not only for its mimicry of black songs and dances but for its cross-dressing as well, a common part of the act. Like carnival and burlesque theater, minstrelsy embodied the issues of its time—among them suffrage, abolition, and political corruption—and made fun of everything from Shakespeare to bourgeois manners.[46] It too has left a legacy in the form of many contemporary entertainment practices (and not just the Ted Danson/Whoopi Goldberg fiasco of recent notoriety). Most important for *Bad Girls*, however, is minstrelsy's ability to mutate across race, class and gender and to make fun of everything, including the white performer's own ethnic origins.

"She who laughs, lasts." —Kate Clinton

Not everyone found mistrelsy amusing. When it comes to humor, there is considerable difference in what people of a given class, race, gender or ethnicity find funny. What makes one person laugh can offend another because different comic sensibilities reflect different experiences and values. It's also because the codes used by particular groups are simply mysterious to those who are not part of them. Humor has many functions; besides serving as entertainment, an escape mechanism, and an expression of subversive intent, it also is used to establish cohesion, solidarity and group identity within specific communities.[47] This is the reason that, say, lesbian humor can be inaccessible to straight women, or that Jewish humor falls flat to those Southerners who have no experience of Jews at all. It is also why many men don't think feminists have a sense of humor. (Perhaps, as June Sochen points out, it's also because we stopped responding to sexist jokes as though they were funny.)

According to Nancy Miller's analysis in *A Very Serious Thing,* American women's humor resembles the humor of any racial or ethnic "minority" in that a dominant theme is "how it feels to be a member of a subordinate group in a culture that prides itself on equality, [trying] to meet standards for behavior that are based on stereotypes rather than on human beings."[48] Humor is thus a way of creating solidarity among the disenfranchised, by bringing the enemy down to size and distancing oneself from one's own oppression.[49]

Humor in the work of *Bad Girls* covers a broad stylistic terrain from irony to slapstick; most of it, though, aggressively makes fun of the ways in which society creates and supports gender inequities. It is the humor of the kitchen and the butcher shop, the bedroom and the boardroom, the tired and the poor. Women's humor at its best creates solidarity within and between groups, challenges traditional role models, defies stereotypes, is seductive, inclusive and, most important, is based on the idea that any and all systems of exploitation, not just those that exploit women, can and must be changed for the better.

Bibbetty Bobbitty Boo

Works of art to which humor is integral, especially if the humor is more slapstick than ironic, are easily dismissed by those who insist on seriousness as integral to "high" art. First of all, not everyone finds the same things funny, so that some pieces simply won't "read" to certain viewers. And, alas, hilarious has been to the artistic canon what the genuinely profane is to the sacred today—a contradiction in terms. This kind of work can also be criticized by some women as "trivializing" important feminist issues by subjecting them to laughter. But effective social critique doesn't exist only in the serious, pure, and reasoned realm of high discourse, despite claims to the contrary.[50]

Artistic production, like cultural production in general, is important because it expresses a society's ordering of its power relationships. As Richard Allen points out in discussing the position of burlesque performers in mainstream culture, all groups within society produce culture, but not all groups are in a position to disseminate their cultural products widely within a society and export them to others, to legitimate and naturalize their tastes in cultural products via social institutions (education, chief among them), or to regulate competing or alternative forms of cultural production via economic power, government policy, and/or legal sanction.[51]

For a brief moment, the wild and wonderful women of early burlesque theater looked as though they might be able to make a real change in the cultural map of mid-nineteenth-century America. But they were nipped in the bud by Victorian moral reformists. However, as even the most inexperienced gardener knows, clipping and pruning, while making a plant *look* dead, are in fact a prerequisite to its later glorious efflorescence. Although carnival and burlesque appeared to give up the ghost, their central qualities have emerged again in the artistic production of today's bad girls. A tendency to go too far, a scathing critique of the status quo, a healthy distain for authority, and pervasive laughter once again characterize an important part of today's artistic production in the hands of women.

The role of the *enfant terrible*, the avant-garde's "inner child," has until now been the province of men, who alone have been allowed to be "bad" in creative and economically productive ways. But women are all too familiar with that *irritable enfant* in a full diaper, and prefer to play with something that's more fun. How about a giant talking Barbie, fully armed, holding Ken's tiny penis aloft and yelling, "Just kidding, folks!"? *("That's <u>not</u> funny!")*

Bad girls like the critical and constructive potential of laughter; they're feeling the intense pleasure of stepping outside the boundaries that, like our mothers' and grandmothers' girdles, have been cutting off our circulation for too long. Their laughter is an antidote to being silenced, defined, and objectified; it resists the construction of an "intelligible, consistent, 'unbroken' story"[52] and opts for the inconsistencies, contradictions and "catch me if you can" elusiveness of multiple narratives. Their laughter is raucous, outrageous, and completely out of hand. Bad girls are hysterical! They'd rather stay mad. And bad.

The backlash of the eighties tried to hold this grinning, hydra-headed, multi-tongued, mutating and menacing specre of feminism at bay, but it looms ever larger on public and private horizons. And now, it's too late. It's here!!! Oh NO. It's......AAARRRGGGHH!!!!!

This essay is dedicated to the memory of my mother, Dorothy Wald Silverman, a.k.a. Dora (1911-1960), to my mother-in-law, Evadne McNeil, and to my daughter, Ruby Dora McNeil, the best of the bad.

1. "Battle of Sexes Joined in Case of Mutilation," *New York Times,* November 8, 1993.

2. Robert Stam, *Subversive Pleasures: Bakhtin, Cultural Criticism, and Film* (Johns Hopkins University Press: Baltimore and London, 1989), p. 9.

3. From *Sense and Momsense* (Doubleday: Garden City and New York, 1986), quoted in Nancy A. Walker, *"A Very Serious Thing": Women's Humor and American Culture* (Minneapolis: University of Minnesota Press, 1988), pp. 35-36.

4. See Frances Bartkowski, *Feminist Utopias* (University of Nebraska Press: Lincoln, Neb., and London, 1988) for a helpful analysis of contemporary utopian novels in general and their relationship to feminism.

5. Mae Gwendolyn Henderson, "Speaking in Tongues: Dialogics, Dialectics, and the Black Women Writer's Literary Tradition," in *Changing Our Own Words: Essays on Criticism, Theory and Writing by Black Women,* ed. Cheryl A. Wall (Rutgers University Press: New Brunswick, N.J., and London, 1989), p. 24.

6. Tania Modleski, "Femininity as Mas(s)querade: a feminist approach to mass culture," in *High Theory/Low Culture: Analyzing popular television and film,* ed. Colin McCabe (St. Martin's Press: New York, 1986), p. 50.

7. Peter Stallybrass and Allon White, *The Politics and Poetics of Transgression* (Cornell University Press: Ithaca, N. Y., 1986), pp. 178, 189.

8. See *The Critical Tradition,* ed. David H. Richter (St. Martin's Press: New York, 1989), p.725.

9. Recent works which also draw on Bakhtin for feminist analysis include Joanna Isaak's essay, "Nancy Spero: A Work in Comic Courage," in the exhibition catalogue *Nancy Spero, Works Since 1950* (Everson Museum of Art: Syracuse, New York, 1987); Mary Russo, "Female Grotesques: Carnival and Theory," in *Feminist Studies/Critical Studies,* ed. Teresa de Lauretis (Indiana University Press: Bloomington, Ind., 1986); and Susan Rubin Suleiman, *Subversive Intent: Gender, Politics and the Avant-Garde* (Harvard University Press: Cambridge, Mass., and London, 1990).

10. Stallybrass and White, *op. cit.,* p.7.

11. The activities of groups like WAC and the Guerrilla Girls have been both effective and unsettling to the status quo in this regard. And their behavior, as well as the costumes, props and masks worn for their demonstrations, are distinctly carnivalesque.

12. Stam, *op. cit.,* p. 86.

13. Stallybrass & White, *op. cit.,* p. 42.

14. Susan Rubin Suleiman, *op. cit.,* p. 4.

15. *Ibid.,* p. 13. Suleiman says that the recurrent tendency of avant-garde or "modern" move-

ments has been to change the way we think about the world by the use of such concepts as "heterogeneity, play, marginality, transgression, the unconscious, eroticism [and] excess." Stallybrass and White *(op. cit.*, p. 177) make a similar point.

16. A recent example is that of Morley Safer, who took the "Emperor's New Clothes" bludgeon to contemporary art on "60 Minutes" (September 19, 1993) by attacking as "worthless junk" abstract painting (Cy Twombley), minimalism (Robert Ryman), artistic strategists (Jeff Koons and Gerhard Richter), conceptual artists (Felix Gonzalez-Torres) and painters and sculptors who use text or images derived from popular sources (Christopher Wool and Robert Gober). Employing the clever and original "my kid could do this" school of argument on Jean-Michel Basquiat's work, Safer bravely denounced the collectors, curators, critics and auction houses who support contemporary art. Notwithstanding the fact that no women artists were even mentioned, and that the transcript of the program refers to a museum docent as a "Whitney Museum lady," Safer's show is a textbook example of how deeply ingrained this particular phobia still is.

17. Stam, *op. cit.*, p. 173. See also Linda Hutcheon, *A Theory of Parody: The Teachings of Twentieth-Century Art Forms* (Methuen: New York and London, 1985).

18. See Henry Louis Gates, Jr., *The Signifying Monkey: A Theory of African-American Literary Criticism* (Oxford University Press: New York, 1988) for a critical and theoretical analysis of the ways in which African-American vernacular traditions have provided a way for black voices to speak for themselves; particularly interesting with regard to *Bad Girls* is his study of the writings of Zora Neale Hurston and Alice Walker. For a discussion of Bakhtin's theories in relation to aspects of black popular culture in Britain, see Paul Gilroy, *"There Ain't No Black in the Union Jack"* (University of Chicago Press: Chicago, 1991).

19. To wit: Rachel Lachowicz's cast-lipstick version of Duchamp's *Urinal* or of Carl Andre's floor pieces; Sherrie Levine's early 1980s series of works "After" Rodchenko, Walker Evans, Leger, Schiele, Kirchner, and others; Deborah Kass's revitalized, Jewish Warhols; Lucy Pul's recasting of Donald Judd's metal stacks, with hair dangling from them; Elayne Sturtevant's meticulously accurate, to-scale replications of paintings by Jasper Johns and others. See Roberta Smith, "The New Appropriationists: Engaging the Enemy," *New York Times*, August 16, 1992.

20. Stallybrass and White, *op. cit.*, p. 57

21. For an excellent summary of the various branches of feminist theory, see Chapter I, "The Discourse of Feminisms: The Spectator and Representation," in Jill Dolan, *The Feminist Spectator as Critic* (UMI Research Press: Ann Arbor, Mich., 1988). Dolan describes the three main branches as follows: "liberal feminism," which demands parity with men under the terms of a general liberal humanism; "cultural feminism," which replaces male power and authority with a female counterpart; and "materialist feminism," which assumes that the polarization of genders is socially constructed and oppressive to both, and emphasizes bringing about change in the system that creates this polarization (p. 15).

22. Stallybrass and White, *op. cit.*, p. 43.

23. *The Portable Dorothy Parker*, introduction by Brendan Gill (Penguin Books: New York, 1944, reprinted 1976), p. 48.

24. Stallybrass and White, *op. cit.*, p. 43.

25. Last year's *Documenta* in Kassel, Germany, for instance, was framed by its organizers as an

international exhibition which purported to deal with "art as a language of its own." Instead, images of naked bodies, sexual organs, hair, excrement, blood, masturbation, corporeal mutilation, procreation, and death threatened to obliterate any artistic excursions into a separate language of art. What the organizers made of all those bodies was most curious to women reading their official statement about the exhibition (see p. 32).

26. Stallybrass and White, *op. cit.*, p. 9.

27. See Mary Russo, "Female Grotesques: Carnival and Theory," in *Feminist Studies/Critical Studies*, ed. Teresa de Lauretis (Indiana University Press: Bloomington, Ind., 1986), p. 219. See also Stallybrass and White, *op. cit.*, p. 65.

28. Leslie Fiedler, *Freaks* (Touchstone Books: New York, 1978), p. 16.

29. *Ibid.*, p. 175.

30. "Extended Sensibilities: The Impact of Homosexual Sensibilities on Contemporary Culture," organized by The New Museum of Contemporary Art, November 29, 1982, at The New School for Social Research, New York.

31. Terence S. Turner, "The Social Skin," in *Reading the Social Body*, ed. Catherine B. Burroughs and Jeffrey David Ehrenreich (University of Iowa Press: Iowa City, 1993), p. 16.

32. Quoted in Stallybrass and White, *op. cit.*, p. 184.

33. *Ibid.*, p. 182.

34. See Stallybrass and White's chapter, "Bourgeois Hysteria and the Carnivalesque," *op. cit.*, pp. 171-190.

35. Elaine Showalter, "The Hysterical Body," a lecture given at The Institute of Fine Arts, New York University, November 11, 1993.

36. See Stallybrass and White, *op. cit.*, p. 174.

37. See Andreas Huyssen, "Mass Culture as Woman: Modernism's Other," in Tania Modleski, *Studies in Entertainment, op. cit.*, p. 195.

38. Robert C. Allen, *Horrible Prettiness: Burlesque and American Culture* (The University of North Carolina Press: Chapel Hill, N. C., and London, 1991), p. 26.

39. Sondra O'Neale, "Inhibiting Midwives, Usurping Creators: The Struggling Emergence of Black Women in American Fiction," in de Lauretis, *Feminist Studies, op. cit.*, p 129.

40. *Art in America's* response to the Morley Safer debacle on "60 Minutes" (see footnote 16) is a case in point: "Although the CBS attack riled some art-world partisans, in the end it could be seen as rather reassuring. Despite reports to the contrary, the gulf between the art world and mass culture is apparently still large enough to make the artistic enterprise worthwhile." (*Art in America*, "Front Page," unsigned, November 1992, p. 37). If this is what makes the artistic enterprise worthwhile, I think I'll drive a cab.

41. Huyssen, *op. cit.*, p. 193.

42. See *Ibid.*, p. 196.

43. Modleski, *op. cit.*, p. 38.

44. Quoted in Margo Jefferson, "The Minstrel Tradition: Not Just a Racist Relic," *New York Times*, October 27, 1993, p. C18, a review of *Blackface Minstrelsy and The American Working Class* by Eric Lott (Oxford University Press: Oxford, 1993).

45. Stam, *op. cit.*, pp. 215-216.

46. See Jefferson, "The Minstrel Tradition," *op. cit.*, p. C18. See also Chapter 6, "The Institutionalization of Burlesque," in Robert C. Allen, *Horrible Prettiness, op. cit.*, for an analysis of the interrelatedness of burlesque and minstrelsy. It is interesting to note that in the nineteenth century female forms of minstrelsy emerged (although the women generally played white characters) that were the result of a hybrid form of the all-male minstrel show and the all-female burlesque theater.

47. See June Sochen, *Women's Comic Visions* (Wayne State University Press: Detroit, Mich., 1991) p. 210.

48. Nancy A. Walker, *"A Very Serious Thing": Women's Humor and American Culture* (Minneapolis: University of Minnesota Press, 1988), pp. x, 29.

49. See Nancy A. Walker, "Towards Solidarity," in June Sochen, *Women's Comic Visions, op. cit.*, p. 58.

50. Stallybrass and White, *op.cit.*, p. 43.

51. Allen, *op. cit.*, p. 31.

52. Suleiman, *op. cit.*, p. 92.

Mother Laughed: The Bad Girls' Avant-Garde

Marcia Tanner

> On Sundays try to walk like a lady and not like the slut you are so bent
> on becoming...this is how to hem a dress when you see the hem com-
> ing down and so to prevent yourself from looking like the slut I know
> you are so bent on becoming...this is how to behave in the presence of
> men who don't know you very well, and this way they won't recognize
> immediately the slut I have warned you against becoming...
> —Jamaica Kincaid, "Girl"[1]

It's hard to know what a bad girl is nowadays. As these exhibitions open,
Hollywood will be releasing a couple of films, each titled (at this writing)
"Bad Girls." Both are about hookers, according to *Los Angeles Times* colum-
nist Alan Citron in his breezy essay "Bumper Crop of Prostitute Films Due."[2]

The first, *Badgirls*, "a Civil War-era tale of a group of prostitutes who try to
track down the thieves who robbed them," sounds like 20th Century Fox's
notion of a "feminist" version of Clint Eastwood's *The Unforgiven* in which
the girls (Andie MacDowell, Mary Stuart Masterson, Madeleine Stowe and
Drew Barrymore) pluckily set out to avenge themselves, sans male hero. In
other words, they're really *good* girls.

In the second *Bad Girls*, from Castle Hill Productions, a "foreigner with
writer's block" moves to New York's Hell's Kitchen to get unblocked via close
study of the prostitutes who work there. (Citron gives no further clues to plot
or subtext, but some of these bad girls are bound to be good girls too, don't
you think?) So why are hookers hot in Hollywood right now? Why is it in
Hollywood's (or the culture's) interests to equate bad girls with prostitutes,
then declaw and defang them, rendering them adorable?

Maybe Hollywood and its avatars justifiably feel a special affinity towards the world's oldest profession? More likely, it's bottom-line stuff.

"There's a plethora of prostitute and pimp projects bouncing around town," Citron observes. "Enthusiasm...apparently springs from the runaway success of 'Pretty Woman,' which has grossed $400 million worldwide. It may also owe to the fact that hookers and pimps, *like cops and doctors*, make for good drama." (My emphasis.)

Pretty Woman, you recall, updates the Pygmalion/Cinderella myths by revealing that all a hard-up hooker needs to blossom into a gracious, lovely, marriageable WASHAP (white Anglo-Saxon heterosexual American princess) are a week in a luxury suite at the Beverly Wilshire Hotel, a few major shopping sprees on Rodeo Drive, and lashings of cash from a greedy tycoon with the nuanced emotional range of a brown paper sack. ("You clean up good," her former colleague tells her.) In other words, she's deemed worthy of metamorphosis from a low-priced commodity to a high-priced one via her innate talent for servicing men, polished by professional skills and aptitude as a quick study, which in turn earns her an enhanced ability to *consume* pricey commodities. Now *there's* a good girl.

If Hollywood wants us to see "bad girls" as whores who are good girls—Heidi Fleiss notwithstanding—that's because (a) it's a titillating yet comforting image that panders to contemporary male and female fears and fantasies; (b) Hollywood's "bad girls," like its cops and doctors, play out their dramas without seriously challenging the patriarchal values and gender caricatures that dominate American society; (c) the dominant point of view, the normative vision, the ways in which women are *seen* and *framed* in Hollywood, literally and figuratively, remains white, male, heterosexual, and mainstream American; and (d) films like this make a lot of folks a lot of money.

Real bad girls however—truly unruly women who threaten to turn the social order upside down—aren't welcome here. They're so terrifying, in fact, that popular culture mythologizes them in films about psychopathic mankillers, evil crones, angry dominatrixes, and monsters possessed by alien or demonic forces. (Can *Unkindest Cut: The Lorena Bobbitt Story* be far behind?) These girls are beyond bad. It's perfectly OK to hate *them*.

Has Hollywood totally co-opted, usurped, domesticated, exhausted and invalidated all the ironic meanings of "bad girls"? No fucking way.

Hollywood's "bad girls" have little in common with the bad girls in these exhibitions. These artists—mostly women plus a few men—are way out of line. They don't care who they offend or what self-evident truths they undermine. They'll laugh at any gender stereotype that someone somewhere holds sacred. Their funniness—and they are, as artist Millie Wilson has remarked, "all kinds of funny"[3]—is perhaps their most transgressive strategy.

"You have to be liberated to laugh," wrote novelist Erica Jong in a 1980 article in *Playboy*.[4] Her point is that a sense of safety and security *vis à vis* mainstream culture may be prerequisite to the confidence required for the radical and open critique of culture that bad girls' laughter represents. But the reverse is also true: laughter is liberating in itself.

Laughter as a tool for liberation is how these "bad girls" use it. Humor for them is both evidence of power and empowering. Their work seduces the viewer via humor, the bracing shock of freedom unleashed by its unexpected, often subtle subversion of accepted rules, and its projection of countervailing versions of experience.

Bad girls have opted for "the license of carnival, a license to overturn, to mimic, and to 'deconstruct'"[5] the ways in which sex and gender are perceived in a male-dominated culture. But unlike at carnival, where misrule reigns only briefly after which everything returns to normal, these unruly artists want to knock permanent dents in society's constructions of gender. Even if they don't succeed in bringing the whole temple crashing down around our heads, they're giving its pillars one hell of a shaking. Their aims are not divisive, restrictive or destructive, though, but expansive and transformative; they invite the viewer to see and think beyond stereotypes and simple either/or oppositions, to imagine a more inclusive, various and funny world.

The original bad girl, the "slut you are so bent on becoming," was the mirror image, implicit or explicit, of the "good girl" our mothers worked so hard to teach us how to be. This good girl template, anxiously imposed on us to ensure our safe navigation through the perilous waters of the patriarchal sea we swam in, was not, we discovered, our mothers' creation. They were channeling the voices of our fathers, their fathers, and their father's fathers, instructing us to be "good girls" in a man's world. If we detected ambivalence in their injunctions—undercurrents of fatalism, anger or rebellion in the lessons they believed it was their duty to impress on us—it was through the

Kim Dingle
Wild Girls (one with glasses & oxfords), 1993

flashes of wit, sarcasm, irony and ridicule that occasionally broke through their act. Mother wit helped save us from turning into uniform lumps of sugar 'n spice.

Good girls, we learned, don't rock the boat. They don't break the rules or radically question absurdities in the social, economic, political or cultural status quo. They don't behave excessively, don't call attention to themselves, never do anything embarassing. They learn ingenious strategies for displaying yet concealing their bodies. They act *feminine*, modestly, quietly, in ways unthreatening to men. They put others' needs and wants first. They may wield power or be aggressive but covertly, through passive manipulation.

Good girls don't talk openly about their own sexual proclivities and erotic fantasies, which are assumed to be heterosexual (male-centered). They don't forge their own persuasive, contradictarian language—verbal, visual, physical—to articulate what they see, think, dream, imagine, feel, desire.

Since many men are alarmed by women with a sense of humor—a live giveaway for a mind and passions of one's own—good girls confine theirs, in the unlikely event they have one, to domestic settings and matters. Good girls don't laugh much in public, never loudly, and certainly not at anything dirty. They're not bawdy, raucous or foul-mouthed. They don't invent their own jokes, don't mock truths held to be self-evident. They don't make fun of men or of men's views of them, not in front of men, anyway. Like Br'er Rabbit, they lay low.

The bad girls in these exhibitions flout all these precepts. As Cyndi Lauper sings, these "girls just wanna have fun."[6] What kinds of mothers did *they* have?

I don't mean the women who actually bore or raised them, who must also be remarkable, judging by the ways their progeny are turning out. I'm talking about the mothers of their inventions. "There always remains in woman that force which produces/is produced by the other—in particular, the other woman," observed Helene Cixous. "The mother, too, is a metaphor."[7]

This essay's title, "Mother Laughed," has two sources whose contrariety makes a useful double metaphor. In her speech accepting confirmation as Justice of the U.S. Supreme Court, Ruth Bader Ginsburg confessed she is notorious in her family for lacking a sense of humor. It's so unusual to hear her laughing, she said, that her daughter began keeping a journal to record those rare occurrences. Its title is *Mother Laughed.*

This story is interesting because Justice Ginsburg is a feminist who has fought passionately and effectively for gender equality in the law throughout her career. One element of her extraordinary success in a male-dominated profession has undoubtedly been the high seriousness revealed in her confirmation hearings, the gravity intrinsic to her personality which thoroughly disarmed (wore out?) her male interlocuters. Displays of female humor in that world might be interpreted as fatal frivolity, disqualifying her from the solemn juridical heights achieved by moral and intellectual heavyweights like Clarence Thomas.

Her daughter, though, loves to hear her laugh out loud; no doubt she would like to hear more of that laughter.

"Imagine the mother laughing," wrote Susan Rubin Suleiman in her book *Subversive Intent: Gender, Politics and the Avant Garde.*[8] Suleiman envisages a mother whose freedom to laugh and play inspires and energizes her daughter: "the mother finally moving, laughing, and playing, a subject...as an enabling myth."[9] She even composes a little drama whose final chorus goes: "Revise, review/ To see things anew/ Teach the daughter to play/ Imagine the mother playing."[10]

It's only in the past 25 years or so that we've begun tracing a matrilineal line for woman artists, since feminist art history and theory began to blossom with the rise of feminism. Women artists of the past were rediscovered; it became conceivable to talk about an actual tradition. Meanwhile, pioneering feminist artists of the 1960s and early 70s were working to define a specifically female art deliberately distinct from mainstream modernism and its perceived misogyny, patriarchal history and arcane inaccessibility. Many women artists subscribed to Lucy Lippard's statement that "the goal of feminism is to change the character of art."[11]

While that goal may persist, its premises have shifted in the two intervening decades. Lippard noticed a change from the early 70s "when feminist artists had been looking for 'shared *images*'" to a quest for "shared *approaches* (political and esthetic)" in the 80s.[12] Artists in the 90s are still exploring many of the same questions 70s artists did—the nature of sexuality, gender identity and representation and formal issues—although their concerns are informed by twenty years of feminist discourse, an enriched "identity politics" encompassing the concerns of gays, lesbians, and people of color, and over a decade of postmodernist artmaking.

Not all female artists, not all feminist artists, not even female artists who deal explicitly with sexual content, are "bad girls" as we're defining that term here. "Our" bad girls have a matrilineage of their own, I believe. A herstory of the bad girl tradition in visual art awaits its chronicler, but dozens of artists have contributed significantly to this uppity heritage. Here I can only touch on a few "laughing mothers" whose inventions have provided important strategies, tools, inspiration and permission for bad girls practicing now.

Until further research uncovers *her* foremothers, the mother of all bad girl artists might have been the Baroque Italian painter Artemisia Gentileschi. Gentileschi was born in Rome just over 400 years ago, on July 8, 1593, but her work was relatively ignored by art historians until this century and really only rediscovered in the 1970s by feminist art history scholars. Mary Garrard's groundbreaking study, *Artemisia Gentileschi*, published in 1989,[13] makes a brilliant case for the consistently female perspective she presented in her compositions, which reworked—and literally *revised* (in the sense of re-envisioned)—traditional themes as they were painted by her male contemporaries.

Her subjects were almost invariably female characters: famous heroic women of antiquity, Biblical or classical, like Susanna, Mary Magdalen, Lucretia, Cleopatra, Esther, and especially Judith, often engaged in dramatic confrontations with men; or allegorical figures, like her quietly revolutionary self-portrait as the Allegory of Painting. Putting a unique spin on these well-worked scenarios, she gave prominence to the female characters, portraying them as powerful, aggressive, vigorous, fully developed human beings endowed with strong will, courage, resolve and minds of their own, who (in Judith's case) are capable of carrying out premeditated acts of violence to defend themselves and free their people. Gentileschi's woman were no shrinking violets.

An artistic prodigy, Gentileschi was taught to paint by her father, the prominent painter Orazio Gentileschi, who also hired fellow artists to complete her training. Always drawn to the most contemporary painting trends, she absorbed the compositional strategies of some of the most eminent artists of her time—Rubens, Cigoli, Vouët, Van Dyck, as well as her father.

Her deepest affinities, though, were with Caravaggio and Michelangelo. The earthy naturalism and highly dramatic compositions and lighting of her canvases owe a lot to Caravaggio; Michelangelo's nuanced pastels inform her palette. But it was in her conception of the female figure—what Garrard calls "her gender-inverted version of androgyny"[14]—that their inspiration is clearest. Artists like Caravaggio, Donatello and Michelangelo "play upon our gender expectations," Garrard points out, "creating cross-gender images that combine elements of each sex in new ways, opening new dimensions of human experience to our imaginative life."[15]

Gentileschi's genius was to re-envisage their male-centered, homoerotic vision of androgyny from a female—even feminist—point of view. Her accomplishment was so radical for its time that it apparently wasn't even recognized; the expressive content of her imagery was somehow masked by her technical virtuosity and command of contemporary styles. In other words, her paintings looked close enough to how people expected paintings to look that she was able to smuggle their subversive content right past her patrons.

Later historians and critics, though, were horrified. "The women in Gentileschi's paintings have frequently been described as 'gory,' 'animalistic,' 'buxom,' and 'sullen,'" observe Rozsika Parker and Griselda Pollock in their book *Old Mistresses*.[16] "Her celebration of great women is characterized as 'irreligious,' and the Judith subjects were described by the nineteenth-century writer, Mrs. Jameson, as 'proof of her genius, and let me add, of its atrocious misdirection.'"[17]

Some writers found Gentileschi's overturning of feminine stereotypes so mind-boggling that they resorted to biographical "explanations." Her allegations of repeated rape by the artist Agostino Tassi (who, ironically, was hired to teach her perspective, which in a way he did), and the humiliation and abuse she suffered at the subsequent trial, proved that she was either an unnatural woman who hated men or a "'lascivious and precocious girl.'"[18]

Gentileschi was a transgressive artist, all right, but was she laughing? Possibly the best answer to that question is to compare her first version of *Judith Slaying Holofernes*, 1612-13—painted shortly after the rape trial—with Caravaggio's *Judith Beheading Holofernes*, 1598-99. The story of Judith, the Jewish heroine who offered herself as hostage to the enemy general Holofernes and beheaded him in his tent, was a popular subject for artists in

Caravaggio's circle. Many versions of it focused on its violent, climactic moment, as do both of these.

Caravaggio's canvas presents us with a delicate maiden who recoils in ladylike distaste as she grasps Holofernes' hair with her left hand while sawing away with the other, daintily holding her sword at arm's length as if bowing a viola da gamba, at an angle offering minimal leverage so that only her slender wrist—which looks barely capable of slicing bread—is engaged in this clearly unfamiliar task. Slightly behind Judith at the composition's extreme right stands her elderly servant, a grim passive witness and shadow figure (in Jungian terms) who holds the cloth ready to receive the head as though performing the role of murder's midwife. Together, they represent the traditional dichotomy of two archetypal aspects of woman, the virgin and the crone.

On the left, the figure of Holofernes rears up on his bed in agony. Only his right arm and shoulder are illuminated with the same intensity as Judith's face and torso, highlighting the helplessness of this virile warrior unmanned by a mere girl. The artist has divided the canvas vertically, separating the two halves with a dark gulf bridged by Judith's arms. This abyss dramatizes her psychological distance from the grisly transaction, as if to dematerialize her involvement and sublime it into the realm of allegory or myth.

Gentileschi's version couldn't be more physical. She makes the bed a prominent stage for the bloody struggle enacted on it, and clusters the three actors in a tightly engaged triangle that fills the entire canvas. The characters are knit together by a tangle of crisscrossed arms; their exposed flesh is brightly illuminated. Holofernes, whose head remains in shadow, is depicted as a large man with massive, meaty biceps, but Judith and her maidservant are equal to him. Similar in age, they're both robust, muscular, attractive young women who work together as a team. They're putting their backs into this, and a lot of energy; their facial expressions reveal nothing but determination and intent concentration on the task at hand.

The servant holds the drunken Holofernes down while Judith wields her sword with the practiced hand of a woman who, back home, has slaughtered goats and lambs for food. She wears a low-cut blue gown that displays the creamy shoulders and swelling breasts of a sensuous, sexually desirable and desirous real woman, neither slut nor idealized saint. Gentileschi's Judith can't be categorized or crammed into anybody's stereotypes. She is who she is. And in this painting, unlike Caravaggio's, the women are definitely on top.

Laura Aguilar
Untitled Self Portrait, 1991

I won't argue that it's a comic picture, but I can't help believing that Gentileschi laughed gleefully while she was painting it and afterwards, when it was finished and released into the world (it's now in the collection of the Museo di Capodimonte in Naples). She knew what she was doing. And there's no question she had a sense of humor that turned on retelling a traditional story from a woman's point of view: in a letter, she once referred to an episode in the legend of the famous Greek hero Perseus as the tale of "Andromeda, when she was freed by a certain knight on the flying horse Pegasus."[19]

Gentileschi's *oeuvre* is, as art historian Leo Steinberg said of Michelangelo's last paintings, "a gift to the twentieth century."[20] Ours is certainly the first era that's able to appreciate the covert meanings and comedic unruliness in her work.

A twentieth-century foremother, the late Swiss artist Meret Oppenheim (1913-1985) was nearly eclipsed by her own precocious brilliance. When her quintessential "Surrealist object" *Déjeuner en fourrure (Luncheon in Fur)*— made in 1936 when she was 23—was first exhibited in Paris, it was bought immediately for the collection of the Museum of Modern Art. It quickly became such a cultural icon, defining an entire artistic movement, that its creator got lost in the shuffle. In the U.S., people assumed "Meret" was a man's name. The artist herself felt oppressed by its fame and even made a parody of the piece later in her career.

Déjeuner en fourrure definitely fulfills the demands of the "Surrealist object" and of the aptly named Dada as well. "If Dadaism really was a product of the impulse to laugh, and Surrealism a consequence of fever, then Meret Oppenheim, with her notion of play, would be somewhere between the two," observes her biographer Bice Curiger.[21] The Surrealist object reworked banal, everyday objects found in the environment, dislocating them from their usual surroundings and functions and often juxtaposing them in weird and unexpected ways. Their role was to disrupt common sense, evoke unease, explode conventional meanings and jolt the viewer into making new and revelatory associations—in effect, to liberate the spectator's imagination (which was assumed to be bourgeois).... Surrealism's "fever" was erotic: the ideal Surrealist object was not only laden with condensed unconscious content, à la Freud, it was also fetishistic, saturated with displaced, often deeply ambivalent and misogynist male desire. Dada objects had to be all those things plus make you laugh.

Luncheon in Fur (or *Lunch in Fur*) is a literal translation of *Déjeuner en fourrure*, the French title given it by Surrealism's arch-Druid (and major misogynist) André Breton. Unlike *Fur-lined Tea Cup*, its usual (euphemistic or just unpoetic?) U.S. translation, it conveys the erotic charge of the work as a sexual pun, as graphic as our homespun "hair pie."

In part, *Déjeuner en fourrure* is a sly parody of the typical Surrealist/Dada object. Both those movements were notoriously dominated by men who treated the women in their lives as doll-like objects born to serve their erotic fantasies, physical needs and—as models and muses—their creative genius. They patronized even the brilliant women artists who joined their circles, often, as in Oppenheim's case, with devastating effect. (Max Ernst wrote a paean to her in which he referred to her as "*Meretlein*," "Little Meret.")

Lunch in Fur comically condenses the domestic, erotic and inspirational functions of the male Surrealist artist's female consort into one convenient, simultaneously seductive and repellent household object. Properly used, it could render his need for an actual woman obsolete, thus freeing her to pursue her own projects, artistic or otherwise. At the same time, it also gives three-dimensional form—perhaps for the first time—to a specifically female experience of erotic pleasure: the fur-lined vessel awaiting the lips, the tongue, the stirring of the spoon....

Déjeuner en fourrure may have been the original feminist Surrealist art object. Transgressive and funny, it alone would qualify Oppenheim as a bad girl. So do several of her other works. *Ma gouvernante–My Nurse–mein Kindermädchen*, also made in 1936, presents a pair of ladies' shoes, their high heels capped with paper frills and "trussed up like lamb chops,"[22] on a silver platter: a concisely witty metaphor for the ideal Surrealist female as nanny, meat, and bride in bondage (with a bit of foot- and shoe-fetishism thrown in). A later work, *The Couple*, 1956, grafts a pair of woman's high-topped lace-up shoes—one with lolling tongue—together at the toe, in a sole kiss that's a droll image of erotic union among equals.

Oppenheim's sneakiest and most prescient expression of gender rebellion may have been, paradoxically, the famous nude photographic portrait of her standing behind and leaning against the massive wheel of a printing press, made by Man Ray in 1933. I say "paradoxically" because nowadays we tend to think of images like this as pure products of the male gaze fastened on the "to-be-looked-atness" of the model. In fact, this was a true collaboration

Lucy Puls
Summa Perfectionis Species (Brooke), 1993

between model and photographer, a "secret joke" they cooked up together.[23] It also uncannily anticipated artist Lynda Benglis's famous *Artforum* ad by forty years (see below).

The image we're familiar with, first published in the Surrealist journal *Minotaure* in 1934 to illustrate André Breton's essay on "convulsive beauty," was cropped at hip level. In that castrated form it perfectly embodies the Surrealist notion of the "mechanical bride," passive, mysterious and self-absorbed, intimately engaging with male machinery (printing press and camera) for the erotic delectation of the male spectator.

In its uncropped version, however, the reading changes dramatically. Titled *Érotique voilée (Veiled Erotic)*, 1933, this print reveals the machinery as an extension of Oppenheim's sinuous, ephebe-like body. The wheel's spokes shield her breasts; the wheel's handle protrudes precisely at groin level, endowing her with an iron phallus. She becomes a hermaphrodite. Thus transformed she raises her arm and hand, coated with printers' ink, to make her mark.

Oppenheim's "gift for sly insurgency," as Nancy Spector calls it,[24] is vividly expressed in this work. In it, she projected an image of female-centered androgyny—of psychological bisexuality in the creative realm—that she believed was necessary if women were to achieve recognition as artists.

"A great work of literature, art, music, philosophy is always the product of a whole person," she said in her acceptance speech for the 1974 Art Award of the City of Basle. "And every person is both male and female. I think it is the duty of a woman to lead a life that expresses her disbelief in the validity of the taboos that have been imposed on her kind for thousands of years," she added. "Nobody will give you freedom, you have to take it."[25]

Even an iron phallus would be an unwelcome appendage, much less no empowering attribute, for Yoko Ono, another natural bad girl foremother. In her 1967 comments *On Film No. 4 (in taking the bottoms of 365 saints of our time*, 1966), Ono wondered "why men can get serious at all."

> They have this delicate long thing hanging outside their bodies, which goes up and down by its own will. First of all having it outside your body is terribly dangerous. If I were a man I would have a fantastic castration complex to the point that I wouldn't be able to do a thing.

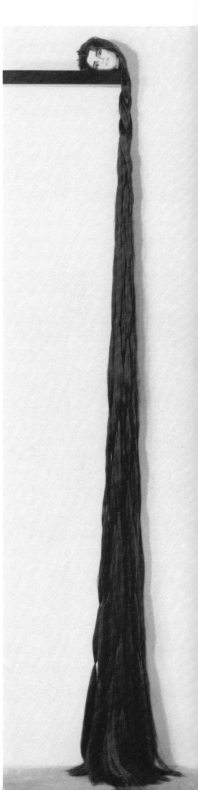

Second, the inconsistency of it, like carrying a chance time alarm or something. If I were a man I would always be laughing at myself. Humour is probably something the male of the species discovered through their own anatomy. But men are so serious. Why? Why violence? Why hatred? Why war?....Men have an unusual talent for making a bore out of everything they touch. Art, painting, sculpture, like who wants a cast-iron woman, for instance?[26]

So much for penis envy and Lacan's *"pas tout."* Since the mid-1950s, Yoko Ono's art has raised disingenuous, iconoclastic challenges like this, questioning conventional notions of sex, gender, sexual morality, pornography, art, imagination, time, space, the mind, reality itself. Working in a variety of forms and media—as performance artist, singer, songwriter and composer, filmmaker, painter, object-maker, and writer—Ono created a body of "wildly subversive"[27] work that fuses Euro-American avant-garde conceptualism of the 60s with an elegantly minimalist Zen Buddhist sensibility. Her projects are enlivened by a deadpan sense of humor camouflaged as innocently whimsical and harmless, like a Zen *koan.* Much of the humor and charge of Ono's work comes from the matter-of-fact, straightfaced decorum whereby she presents the radically outrageous off-the-wallness of her content.

Believing that art and life are inextricable, she's been daring in both. Through her own art work made in the 1960s and in her later collaborations with John Lennon—after their marriage thrust her into the public eye and effectively put a stop to "the quiet conceptual games I was playing"[28]—she made herself visible, vulnerable, and rebellious in ways virtually unthinkable for a woman of her background.

Ono was raised to be a traditional Japanese woman, submissive, repressed and obsessively polite. Born in Tokyo into an aristocratic banking family, she grew up in a rigidly conservative, privileged household, where, she has said, "the creative needs of women were basically ignored." A move to Scarsdale, New York with her family in 1951, where she enrolled in Sarah Lawrence College, apparently gave her the impetus to break loose and reinvent herself.

Stifled by her classical art training, she quit school before earning her degree and began making "instruction pieces," the spare, deceptively innocent, miniature depth bombs for the mind that became central to her *oeuvre.* Written recipes for performing actions and making conceptual music compositions, paintings, films, poetry and other life/art projects, Ono's instruction pieces are definitely *koan*-like. They're designed to activate readers' awareness of the world around them, provoke meditation and poetic connections and liberate creative potential. Instead of presenting a finished object, the instructions invite the viewer to complete the piece imaginatively—to become, in effect, the artist of a work that will be realized differently in the experience of each beholder. Most of them use humor to spark enlightenment. "Draw a map to get lost," suggests a 1964 piece.[30]

To gauge how subversive these works were, recall that Ono was making them when Abstract Expressionism had displaced all the available air in the contemporary art establishment. The cult of the heroic male artist—individual geniuses whose grand gestural canvases were not only original, monumental "masterworks" but also highly valuable commodities—was at its height.

Sharing conceptual art's rejection of the art object as commodity, Ono's instruction pieces were an implicit critique of the concept of ownership, either as creator or collector. Like the teachings of her mentor, the late composer, artist and writer John Cage, these pieces suggest that artmaking is a process of attentiveness to nature and the motions of the mind, of imaginative play and revery; that art exists in time and individual experience, not necessarily in space; that the artist's role is that of catalyst or facilitator since every person is potentially an artist and therefore potentially free.

Ono also viewed her work, in the Buddhist tradition, as an offering or gift. The Japanese way of gift-giving is to offer one's best while denying or downplaying the gift's value. Ono's instruction pieces, like all her work, arrived at a formal equivalent of that contradictory goal.

Some instruction pieces were fairly explicit feminist jabs at the art world—for instance "KITE PIECE II" of 1963:

> *Every year on a certain day, collect*
> *old paintings such as De Kooning, Klein,*
> *Pollack.* [sic]
> *Make kites with them and fly.*
> *Fly them high enough and cut the strings*
> *so they will float.*

And, PAINTING TO BE WORN (1962):

> *Cut out jackets or dress from acquired*
> *paintings, such as Da Vinci, Raphael,*
> *De Kooning. You may wear the painted*
> *side in or out.*
> *You may make underwears* [sic] *with them as well.*[31]

In New York in the early 60s, Ono became involved with Fluxus, a group of radical international artists whose work brought together the ideas of Marcel Duchamp, Dada and Cage. She made a number of performances under the Fluxus banner, some of them fiercely feminist in content.

In *Cut Piece*, performed in 1964 in Tokyo and a year later at Carnegie Hall in New York, she invited members of the audience to cut off pieces of her clothing (she always wore her best suit) as she sat impassively on the stage, enduring this ritual of symbolic yet actual assaults until she was nearly naked. The work's impact derived from the cumulative effect of those repetitive actions over time. At first innocuous, even playful, their character gradually mutated into a threatening exchange of power. "As one by one, men and women snipped off more and more of her suit and underclothing the tension mounted," observed a New York critic. "An adolescent boy came up and amputated her bra, by which point most of the audience were possessed by fear and anxiety and realized they were trapped by the piece."[32]

Ono's inspiration for *Cut Piece* was the legend of the Buddha, who had renounced his life of privilege to wander the world, giving whatever was asked of him. His soul achieved supreme enlightenment when he allowed a tiger to devour his body, and Ono saw parallels between the Buddha's selfless giving and the artist's. When addressing serious issues—in this case voyeurism, sexual aggression, gender subordination, violation of a woman's personal space, violence against women—Ono invariably found means to combine dangerous confrontation with poetry, spirituality, personal vulnerability, and edgy laughter.

Rape (or Chase), a film she made in collaboration with John Lennon in 1969, is thematically related to *Cut Piece*; it also deals with voyeurism and the invasion of personal space. Here, though, it refers most directly to the couple's hounding by the media after their marriage in 1968. Ono cast the cameraman and soundman as assailants whose assault weapons are their remarkably phallic film camera and microphone. Their prey is a young woman they stalk on the street. The pursuit begins as a lighthearted game and the woman is at first amused by the men's attention. She becomes increasingly disturbed by their relentlessness as they follow her home, however, and finally turns on them in rage and terror as they corner her. The film's ambiguous status—is it staged or *cinéma vérité*?—contributes to its strong emotional impact.

Ono's best known *Film No.4 (Bottoms)*, made in England in 1966, satirized the Puritanical notion that the naked human body is obscene and gave England's rigid censorship laws a cheeky slap on both cheeks. An injunction against its commercial release was issued, in fact, and later overturned.

As in *Cut Piece* and her musical compositions, the film set up a framework for a repetitive action: in this case, sequential, straightforward images of 365 pairs of moving buttocks (the subjects walked in place), each filling and dividing the screen into a fleshy four-part grid. The cumulative, totally non-erotic effect of *Bottoms'* simplicity of means, matter-of-fact presentation, and the repetitive rhythmic movement of the images was, as Ono intended, to point up the absurdity of censoring images of the human body. The work also comments metaphorically on repression of difference and expression in society at large.

For the soundtrack, Ono recorded the conversations that went on in the studio while the film was being shot. The contrast between the purity of the onscreen images and the pretentious dialogue (someone once described the British as "neurotically articulate and psychologically naive") set up a cognitive dissonance that intensified Ono's point.

Ono uses simple means and language to create complex, multilayered experiences. Her work evokes contradictory responses that keep the audience uneasy and off-balance, in a state of bemused not-knowing, and laughter is its most unsettling ingredient. Every one of her pieces can be read as a subtle joke on some aspect of Western society's unexamined axioms and the entrenched sign systems that reinforce them—what the feminist writer Gayatri Spivak calls "semiotic fields." Never overtly didactic, Ono sets up ambiguous situations that allow the spectator to make his/her own judgments and imaginative leaps. Semiotic fields forever.

Curator Elizabeth Armstrong of the Walker Art Center in Minneapolis credits Ono with being "one of the key figures in the sexual revolution of the

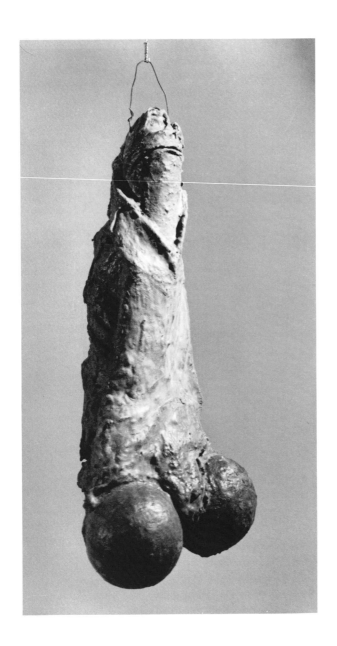

Louise Bourgeois
Fillette, 1968

60s....People think Yoko rode on John's coattails, but I think it was the opposite. Lennon seemed like a man who'd worked himself into a corner, and his partnership with Yoko gave him a whole new life."[33] This may be a tactful way of saying that their collaborations looked a lot more like Ono than Lennon, which in fact they did.

Writer Kristine McKenna cites a 1992 article by Kristine Stiles in the journal *Art Criticism* that "makes a plausible case for the idea that Lennon's transformation from a macho, working-class bloke and spoiled pop star into an ardent feminist and political activist was one of Ono's greatest creative acts."[34]

And an inspiration to bad girls everywhere.

Sculptor Louise Bourgeois, like Yoko Ono, seems to have been born a renegade and menace to society. In a less permissive era, she would probably have been burned as a witch long before she reached her present age of 82. The Inquisition would have had no mercy on a woman with her uncanny access to the secret recesses of the psyche, much less her ability to bring her dark discoveries into the light and mold them, like a shaman's spirit bundles, into magical, sexually charged physical forms.

One look at her terrifying tableau *Destruction of the Father*, 1974—a cave-like (mouth-like, womb-like, *vagina dentata*-like?) chamber whose latex and plaster interior bulges with breast and tooth-shaped protuberances and displays a table laden with what appear to be animal remains—and those Inquisitors would *know* she'd slept with the Devil. Women don't have fantasies of murderous rage against the patriarch, let alone express them so viscerally and violently, unless they're possessed. Do they?

Luckily, Bourgeois came fully into her own as an artist in the 1970s when feminism was on the rise, at a time when art audiences sought relief from the arcane austerities and inaccessibility of postminimalism and Conceptualism and the lack of personal, emotional content in art. Although she'd been making and showing her work since the 1940s, the mainstream art establishment finally caught up with her when Neo-Expressionism hit. Last year she represented the United States in the Venice Biennale; she was in Documenta the year before.

As a witch (her practice matches at least one contemporary definition of witchcraft[35]), Bourgeois is a naturally bad girl, but she brings additional credentials to her role as foremother.

Throughout her career Bourgeois has pursued an idiosyncratic path, making art that followed its own inner logic and psychological imperatives independent of (though not oblivious to) art world isms. Critics complained that she was unclassifiable, that her evolution failed to progress in any normal linear fashion and couldn't be parsed, art historically. She was an outlaw.

Rooted in twentieth-century geometric abstraction in the line of Arp, Brancusi, Giacometti, Moore and Hepworth, she mined Surrealism to develop her own idiom, one that allowed her to tap the contents of her own unconscious and find means of representing directly and symbolically what she found there. She began developing a vocabulary of sexually allusive forms—phallus-like, breast-like, clustered or freestanding columnar shapes, nest-like shapes pierced with holes—that she revisited obsessively, continually recombining and reconfiguring them, drawing out more and more of their possibilities.

In the beginning her work was laden with homesickness, anxiety and a sense of vulnerability and isolation, often relieved by wry humor. One early series, made in the 40s after she moved from her native France to New York and before she began making sculpture, was her *Femme Maison (Woman House)* drawings. These replaced women's heads, sometimes bodies too, with houses. Disturbing yet whimsical, the images reveal the dreadful realization of a newly married female artist that she may have traded her identity for the pleasures and terrors of domestic comfort.

It would be another twenty years before Bourgeois returned to such overt expressions of feminist concerns, although a wonderful 1950 drawing of a winged vagina (the wings are also covered with pubic hair) shows that she was thinking about them. Anthropomorphized architecture and the themes of house as home, shelter, womb and refuge recur, however, throughout her *oeuvre*.

Bourgeois grew more audacious as she aged. When Surrealist intellectuality and detachment couldn't contain the raw, elemental urgency of her taboo subject matter any longer, her work became more expressionistic. In the 60s she began experimenting with new materials. Formerly she'd worked in wood; now she wanted pliability, malleability. She tried plaster, plastics, latex rubber, cement, marble, bronze, and made a phenomenal variety of work. Her sculptures oscillated between objects that verged on the formless (they were called "anti-form" at the time; I would call them metamorphic, *trans-form*), and more coolly classical compositions. In general, they resisted neat classification. Themes that emerged in this period, besides her primary one of the self and others, included: "woman and self-image; pregnant woman; human body shaped as a weapon; human body in relation to nature; body parts as isolated shapes; weapons, skeins, tapestry shuttles, nests; fecundity, nurturing, food; landscape, earth, topography; growth, seeds, sprouting; the terrain of the unconscious; hiding, protection, inner sanctums; mystery, fear, pain, anger; the human world in relation to the animal world; individuals, groups, families; balance and harmony; formlessness and loss of control."[36]

This roster reads almost like a thematic shopping list for the next three generations of women artists. Since Bourgeois wasn't hampered by current feminist debates over the woman-as-metaphor-for-nature problem, she played guiltlessly with every imaginable combination, permutation and metamorphic analogy among the above.

Bourgeois condenses male and female sexual imagery into forms resembling primitive fertility sculptures. There are swelling, fecund phallic breasts (*Trani Episode*, ca. 1971-72); pendulous, weighty breasts which are also plump scrota or clusters of fruit (*Untitled* ink drawing, 1948-51); a hugely pregnant woman with a phallus for a head (*Harmless Woman*, 1969). A slender, sensuously abstracted female figure, headless and armless, turns its vulnerable body into a dangerous weapon (*Femme Couteau, Knife Woman*, 1969-70); a detumescent penis, sculpted tenderly in marble, becomes a metaphor for rest and regeneration (*Sleep, II*, 1967).

Bourgeois's work is full of visual (and sometimes verbal) puns on sexual forms. Six little bronze phalluses in broad-brimmed hats (one's a dwarf) look like animated mushrooms *and* a group of chatty French clerics (the slang term for condom in French is *petit chapeau*, little hat; *Untitled*, ca. 1970-72). The grotesque and very droll *Fillette (Little Girl)*, 1968—a two-foot high latex phallus and scrotum, suspended by its petit chapeau and swaddled in its fore-skin—is so unaccountably sweet and has such presence that you really do want to cuddle this outrageous object like a baby. In *Femme-Maison '81 (Woman House '81)* Bourgeois sculpted an enigmatic scenario in black marble that a viewer might find nightmarish, comforting, amusing, or any combination thereof. It is a small, isolated clifftop house surrounded by a fecund forest, a sexualized landscape of giant swaying phalluses, cloaked guardians/captors that also suggest seed pods or ova bursting from Fallopian stalks.

Bourgeois's work is ghost-haunted; it reclaims and transforms emotion-laden childhood memories into ambiguous icons, personages and tableaux fraught with anxiety and passion. She has used her art all along as an instrument for self-discovery, exorcism, power, and growth. In that sense it is personal and autobiographical. But because the formal vocabulary she's invented has its roots in such primordial, almost archetypal, imagery it transcends her individual experience. She's found sculptural equivalents for previously inaccessible, specifically female motions of the psyche, as felt through the female body, that communicate to any gender.

Her works trigger powerful unconscious associations or play upon the mind like the imagery in dreams. They open up new possibilities for transformation, metamorphosis, insight and play in the external world. Like a true witch—a laughing witch who views life as tragic and darkly humorous—she "dissolves dualities and sees opposites as complements."[37] That she enables us to do the same through her work is her special genius.

Faith Ringgold has been a seriously successful troublemaker since the 1960s. Both in her art and in the real-world arena of civil rights activism she has fought against racial and gender stereotyping, injustice and inequities in U.S. society throughout her career. And she has never stopped fighting for racial and gender equality and equitable representation in museums for women artists and artists of color. "Everything about my life has to do with the fact that I am a black woman," she has said.[38]

Her tactics have changed over the years. From guerrilla warfare, outright confrontation and overt expressions of rage and anguish in her art and life, Ringgold has moved to the subtler, more subversive strategy of infiltrating the system from within. When she began making her "story quilts" in 1983, Ringgold chose the bad girl route, using humor and sensory seduction to smuggle explosive material past the guards into the heart of the citadel. Paradoxically—or maybe not, since it allowed her to speak with her own authentic voice, always the most convincing—she accomplished this by rejecting white men's tropes and using gifts she was given by her own heritage. Her story quilts are her great legacy to the bad girl tradition.

Ringgold was a painter to begin with, laboring to represent black experience, black people and black history using the techniques of Euro-American modernist painting she learned in art school. An early painting, *Flag for the Moon: Die Nigger*, 1969—in which the stripes of the American flag covertly spell out the racial taunt—is a powerfully graphic, scathing indictment of the skewed priorities of a society that could spend millions on the space program while short-changing its own citizens of color.

Frustrated by the limits of the medium to express what she saw and felt, in the 70s she began making life-sized three-dimensional figures of black people, based on actual people she had known in Harlem where she grew up and still lives. "I decided to experiment," she said. "To stop denying the part of me that loves making things with cloth."[38] Collaborating with her mother, the fashion designer Willi Posey, she sewed them out of fabric and used beading, tie-dyeing, needlepoint and other African or Euro-American women's crafts to realize each personage.

The first of these marvelously expressive, animated figures looked more like African tribal sculptures than representational portraits of African-Americans. As they evolved and grew more three-dimensional, though, the soft sculptures took on the lineaments of recognizable American types. In *The Wake and Resurrection*, 1976, Ringgold created the tableau of "Moma and Nana," two matronly black women garbed in black, mourning "Bena and Buba." The young black-shrouded couple lie on their funeral bier, a red, black and green "Flag Pad" bordered with white shells. The figures' inky blackness is relieved only by touches of white and red, most dramatically on the faces of the mourners which are masks of grief.

This narrative grouping carries a tremendous emotional charge. Ringgold made the characters and their emphatic blackness both individual and emblematic. A scene of tragedy within a specific family, it also represents the mourning of all African-American mothers for their endangered children.

Ringgold's "story quilts" evolved from the paintings on cloth (tankas) she had been making throughout the 70s. They grew out of her "need to tell stories not with pictures or symbols alone, but with words,"[40] as well as her desire to focus on black women's experience. She "realized that...quilts, so intimately connected with women's lives, could become a most effective vehicle for telling the stories of their lives."[41]

Quilts also link her to her own family history. Ringgold's great-grandmother, Betsy Bingham, sewed quilts as she had been taught by *her* mother, Susie Shannon, a slave who made quilts for the family that owned her. Ringgold has also borrowed ideas from the separate African-American tradition of quiltmaking—improvisational and polyrhythmic, like jazz—as well as African modes of quiltmaking that incorporate written imagery and ancient geometric patterns.

Her first story quilt, *Who's Afraid of Aunt Jemima?*, 1983, is a fictional revision of the "most maligned black female stereotype" to "reveal the true story never before told." Ringgold retells the saga of the *real* Jemima Blakey and the large family she supports as a contemporary success-in-business story. In this version—part tongue-in-cheek, part wish-fulfillment fantasy, part inspirational tract—there's no trace of the genial black mammy, purveyor of pancakes and warm, uncensorious nurturer of the white American family. This Jemima is one tough broad.

Ringgold's early quilts mingled blocks of handwritten texts with images painted directly onto a handsewn quilted canvas surface, bordering them with patchworks of bright patterned fabrics. Some of the narratives are long and complex, even (as in the later *Bitter Nest Series*, 1988) covering several quilts like installments in a serialized family saga. They mix autobiographical material with fiction and fantasy, combining elements of the African and West Indian "dilemma tale" with folklore and anecdote.[42]

In the mid 80s the quilts opened out, leaving a large central area for Ringgold's vividly painted *faux naif* images—Grandma Moses and Romare Bearden meet Joan Brown and Marc Chagall—with texts confined to narrow borders at top and bottom, as in *Tar Beach*, 1988. The five quilts in the *Woman on a Bridge* series of 1988 eliminate text altogether; Ringgold lets the imagery tell the fantastic story of women taking possession of the bridges of New York and San Francisco; those "magnificent masculine structure[s]," as Ringgold calls them, which to her also resemble suspended quilts.

Woman Painting the Bay Bridge shows a young airborne black woman, nude except for her hair ribbon, applying red paint to the bridge connecting San Francisco with the largely African-American East Bay. The overall image is of exhilarating freedom, but red paint the color of blood has dripped down the side of the paint can she carries, obscuring the "T" in "paint." *Dancing on the George Washington Bridge*, 1988, has a group of lively, good-looking young

Faith Ringgold
#3 The Picnic at Giverny, 1991

black women in brief dresses—like the world's biggest girl group—dancing in the air above the bridge strung like an intricate harp behind them. It's a wonderfully attractive vision.

Ringgold's newest quilts, *The French Collection, Part I*, were first shown in 1992. They tell the fictional story of a young black woman named Willa Marie Simone who goes to *fin de siècle* Paris to study art. Seeing this period of art history through Willa's eyes gives Ringgold license to rewrite the master narrative visually, and she does so with tremendous verve and wit.

In one quilt, Willa Marie is Picasso's model, posing in his cluttered studio beneath the gaze of *Les Demoiselles d'Avignon* and the African masks that inspired his "masterpiece." *The Sunflowers Quilting Bee at Arles* places illustrious women of African-American history—Mary McLeod Bethune, Sojourner Truth, Rosa Parks and others—together in a field of sunflowers, where they're piecing a sunflower-patterned quilt. Van Gogh stands off to one side, holding a bunch of sunflowers and looking on.

Art critic Roberta Smith called this piece a "tribute to female solidarity and individual struggle" whose "contrasting depictions of the quilted sunflowers and the painted sunflower field...make their own political point in purely visual terms....The artist juxtaposes the solitary, traditionally male activity of painting with the collective, traditionally female one of quilting, while fusing their different visual effects into a single work of art."[43]

In this series as in her other story quilts, Ringgold mixes appropriation, pattern painting, portraiture, sewing, history, personal narrative, African, African-American and European-American artistic and cultural forms, rich textiles, gorgeous colors and complex designs—a transgressive hybrid if there ever was one—to make mordant points about the politics of race and gender. By rewriting history from a highly personal African-American feminist perspective, the quilts radically revise the "massa narrative."

Ringgold's quilts have helped legitimize traditional women's crafts and methods—sewing, quilting, dollmaking, pattern and decoration—as valid media for making art. They affirm the value of the matrilineal line, the strength to be found in what she refers to as "the family of women." They're funny, beautiful, accessible, and absolutely right on. Faith Ringgold is one helluva foremother.

Sculptor Lynda Benglis took a different segment of art history's master narrative—the one she happened to be immersed in herself—and tackled it like the big macho bull it was. She may have been the first American woman artist to parody and invert contemporary male artists' most lugubrious productions with her own brand of formal mockery.

In the late 1960s and early 70s, when Minimalism dominated the art world, Benglis was working with huge environmental installations of poured, pigmented polyurethane foam. The antithesis of everything Minimalist sculptors (who were all male) stood for, these were ferocious-looking free-form excrescences that often jutted from the walls like gigantic mutant crustacea or weird rock formations and had a powerful, primordial physical presence.

Benglis used the same material to make blobby formless "pours" and dedicated a particularly disgusting one, a brown cascade of what looked like uncooked chocolate pudding or worse, topped with a lesser flow of darker fudge sauce, to Mr. Minimalism himself, Carl Andre (*For Carl Andre*, 1970). Benglis also lampooned Jackson Pollock's work in her poured latex floor paintings. Using Pollock's pouring technique, she called hers "Fallen Paintings" and left them where they lay, like rubber Pollock compositions that had slithered off their canvases and been run over by a steamroller.

What Benglis objected to was first of all the difficulty she was having being recognized in the male-dominated art world. That wasn't only *her* problem. Her deeper argument, though, was philosophical: she was temperamentally averse to the rigid either/or categories, the mutually exclusive, yes/no on/offs of traditional Western male "rationality," whether expressed formally in art or behaviorally, in attitudes toward gender. Like Louise Bourgeois, Benglis consistently eluded categorization in her work and her being, seeking novel modes of inclusivity that undermine traditional polarities. But she did this with a theatrical flair, a degree of bold insouciance, mischief and daring that might have made the shy Bourgeois recoil.

Both artists shared an interest in androgyny expressed through formal means. A series of pieces Benglis made in the late 70s were inspired by her fascination with masquerade and the flamboyant gay parades at Mardi Gras in New Orleans, where she grew up. One of these, the floozyish *Lagniappe: Bayou Babe*, 1977, is a wall piece consisting of a stocky, slightly bent pole wrapped in bands of brightly colored glitter, topped and tailed by irridescent polypropylene flounces studded with reflecting discs. It looks exactly like a phallus in

drag, and although not as cuddly as Bourgeois's *Fillette* it has some of that work's ridiculous charm.

Talk of endearing phalluses brings us inevitably to the work that earned Benglis a permanent, gold-leaf-lined niche in the Bad Girls' Hall of Fame. I'm referring, of course, to her ad in the November 1974 issue of *Artforum,* for which she posed belligerently, hand on hip, wearing nothing but sunglasses and flaunting an enormous dildo. (A previous invitation for one of her solo gallery exhibitions featured her nude self-portrait from the rear.)

An intentionally outrageous provocation, the ad represented a big "Up yours" to the art establishment and its indifference to women artists, while satiriz-ing—and taking to its logical conclusion—the media marketing of macho male art stars like her own sometime collaborator Robert Morris. The ad also co-opted the male gaze. Benglis stares out boldly at the viewer, making sub-ject and object indistinguishable.

In carnivalesque mode, the ad also underlined the integrative impulses that inform Benglis's work. By assuming an androgynous persona in its most extreme physical manifestation, as an exceptionally well-endowed hermaph-rodite, Benglis truly advertised the intentions and preoccupations of her art. Naturally the ad offended almost everybody and caused a tremendous brouhaha, just as it was meant to do. Thanks, Mom.

Barely 41, Cindy Sherman is too young to be a *Bad Girls'* mom—many artists in these exhibitions are older than she is—but her work is so important and central to this project that I'm including her, my final entrant, as an honorary stepforemother: yet one more fictive role for her to represent.

Since the late 70s Sherman has become known for her increasingly outra-geous, invariably arresting photographs which, until recently, have been of herself. These are not in any sense self-portraits though they are about identity. Sherman doesn't consider herself primarily a photographer; rather, she's a conceptual artist who may work as film director, set designer, makeup technician, performance artist, photographer and painter on any given pro-ject. Like many of her contemporaries, she uses the camera as a tool to explore the nature of representation itself, and to expose the fiction of the photograph as a faithful gauge of reality.

Sherman's photographs are about image-making and the ways in which media-made imagery—in TV, movies and advertising—presents us with altered versions of the world that are more compelling, more coercive, more convincing than our own unmediated perceptions. Her work reveals the chilling vacuity of those chimaerae. She makes us confront the media's ability to project such seductive images, and learn to recognize the artifice they deploy in order to manipulate our desire for those illusions and incite our longing to possess and have power over them—even, or especially, if that means having to *buy* something these images are selling, onto which we can displace our frustrated desire.

Photographs are dangerous; they really do steal the souls of viewer and subject both. Sherman wants to show us just how dangerous they are. Her work provokes us to question how photographs create us, shape our self-images, particularly if we are women subjected to the male gaze of photographers and viewers alike. She does this by constantly subverting the conventions of the kinds of photographs she parodies, continually undermining the viewer's expectations as a result. She presents us with photographs that are never exactly what they seem to be, and even what they seem to be is often difficult to fathom.

Her black and white "film stills" (1977-80) look almost enough like the real thing to pass, but not quite. They don't refer to any actual, specific films although they might (mis)lead us to believe they do. Most people probably can guess that they are fictional tableaux—as a lot of real film stills were, in fact (they were often reenactments or completely invented scenes that weren't actually in the movie). The actual status of Sherman's "stills" on the reality-to-fiction scale raises disquieting questions. They're plausible and appealing yet puzzling. Are they imitations of specific scenes? Reproductions? Camp parodies? Fictional versions of fictions? Representations of representations? Reminiscent of scenes from Hollywood B movies and classic *film noir* of the 50s and 60s, the "stills" present Sherman, wearing different wigs, costumes and makeup, as a variety of stock female characters. There's the country girl in dirndl skirt and sneakers waiting for her ride into town (*Untitled Film Still # 48*, 1979); the fresh-faced young thing newly arrived in the big city (*Untitled Film Still #23*, 1978); the blowsy Shelley Winters type weeping into the dregs of her Manhattan (*Untitled Film Still, #27*, 1979). Needless to say, films with characters like these were directed and photographed by men.

Camera angles, settings, props, and Sherman's detached, deadpan portrayals make these pieces profoundly atmospheric. They all evoke a nebulous nostalgia, a fuzzy sense of *déjà vu*, unfocused longing, indefinable loss; they set up expectations that they can't fulfill. The nostalgia may just be for old movies. It may also register our recognition that seeing (and believing in) female characters in films from a single—read masculine—point of view is no longer viable, thanks to Sherman's reclamation of the terrain.

Ditto with Sherman's color "Centerfold" series of 1981. These exploit the wide, horizontal format of the *Playboy* centerfold to produce a remarkable group of closeups printed life size (2′ x 4′) and shot mostly from above, so that Sherman's characters seem pinned down and trapped, tightly cropped inside their frames and romantically lit. The spectator looms over the images of these adolescent girls, looking down on them from the power position. It's easy to fantasize them as within grasp.

That advantage would gain the viewer little with these young women. Apart from being female, they have nothing in common with the standard centerfold. Instead of passive narcissists or extroverted exhibitionists inviting the viewer's erotic projections, these are problematic females—tense, anxious, awkward, anguished. They crouch or sprawl; they're disheveled, damp, sweaty, dirty. One looks as through she's just been saved from drowning, perhaps against her will. Resistant to desire, these are girls only a mother could love.

Sherman's "Fashion" series of 1983-84 is an utter travesty of fashion photography's conventions. Funny and completely deadpan, these life-sized, luridly colored prints show Sherman multiply disguised and wearing a variety of truly bizarre outfits. All of them look like some kind of hideous drag, although nothing any real self-respecting drag queen would wear. Every character appears to be demented or eccentric in a different but equally disturbing way. This is glamor forced to its knees, made to grovel and howl for mercy. "I'm disgusted with how people get themselves to look beautiful," Sherman said of this series, "I'm much more fascinated with the other side."[44]

Sherman's photographs have the disquieting quality of still life, more accurately *nature morte*, dead nature, as the French call it. A null blankness, an airless silence, pervades even her most charged images. Each ambiguous tableau simultaneously implies and denies the possibility of a narrative; you really can't (*I* can't, anyway) penetrate them or imagine a before or after for any of them although they tempt you to.

How Sherman achieves this uncanny sense of total arrest, of nothing happening to no one nowhere in nontime, is a mystery to me. She does, though. Every image contains plenty to look at but there's really nothing there. Even the memories they trigger are illusory. With her film stills, for instance, people often tell Sherman they remember the movie her image came from, when "in fact I had no film in mind at all."[45]

Sherman uses the image of the woman as the exemplary object to be photographed. Playing the actress playing her various self-assigned roles, Sherman's presence in the finished print is as a replica of a replica. By placing herself many removes from the viewer, she takes control of her image and deflects the viewer's gaze away from herself as the object of desire toward the mechanisms engendering that desire.

The artists in *Bad Girls* and *Bad Girls West* have taken the examples of their foremothers to heart. Some make work that's parodic and satirical, "humoring" male tropes; some mischievously rewrite or revise the "master" scripts from a different point of view. Others invent new narratives, images and metaphors, new modes of representing and projecting their own specifically female experience—formally, stylistically, technically, conceptually—that circumvent paternal constructs altogether.

This is perhaps the ultimate transgression, the most subversive laughter of all. Not only do these artists disobey explicit commandments enjoined by the fathers and handed down through the mothers' complicity, they ignore the entire myth of male hegemony, of paternal lawgivers in art and everywhere else. They've freed themselves with such spirited irreverence, such conviction and assurance, that male artists are now imitating *them*.

Girls just wanna have fun.

1. Jamaica Kincaid, "Girl," in *At the Bottom of the River* (Aventura: New York, 1985), pp. 3-5.

2. Alan Citron, "Bumper Crop of Prostitute Films Due," *Los Angeles Times*, November 3, 1993.

3. In a conversation at Ruth Bloom Gallery, Los Angeles on July 23, 1993.

4. Erica Jong, "You Have to be Liberated to Laugh," *Playboy*, April 1980, p. 162. Cited by Alice Sheppard, "Social Cognition, Gender Roles, and Women's Humor," in *Women's Comic Visions*, ed. June Sochen (Wayne State University: Detroit, 1991), p.78.

5. Judy Little, "Humoring the Sentence: Women's Dialogic Comedy," in *Women's Comic Visions*, *op. cit.*, p. 19.

6. *Girls Just Want to Have Fun*, music and lyrics by Robert Hazard, New York, Sony Tunes, Inc., 1983. Recorded by Cyndi Lauper, 1983.

7. Hélène Cixous, "The Laugh of the Medusa" (extract), in *Modern Feminisms: Political, Literary, Cultural*, ed. Maggie Humm (Columbia University Press: New York, 1992), p. 200.

8. Susan Rubin Suleiman, "Feminist Intertextuality," in *Subversive Intent: Gender, Politics and the Avant-Garde* (Harvard University Press: Cambridge, Mass. and London, England, 1990), p. 179.

9. Suleiman, *op. cit.*, p. xvi.

10. Suleiman, *op. cit.*, p. 10.

11. Lucy Lippard, "In the Flesh: Looking Back and Talking Back," in *Backtalk* (exhibition catalogue, Contemporary Art Forum: Santa Barbara, Cal., 1993), p. 5.

12. Lippard, *op. cit.*, p. 6.

13. Mary D. Garrard, *Artemisia Gentileschi* (Princeton University Press: Princeton, N. J., 1989).

14. *Op. cit.*, p. 7

15. *Ibid.*

16. Roszika Parker and Griselda Pollock, *Old Mistresses: Women, Art and Ideology* (Pantheon Books: New York, 1981), p. 21.

17. *Ibid.*

18. *Ibid.* , quoting Margot and Rudolf Wittkower (no futher citation).

19. Garrard, *op. cit.*, p. 10; see also Appendix A # 28.

20. Quoted in Garrard, *op. cit.*, p. 8.

21. Bice Curiger, *Meret Oppenheim: Defiance in the Face of Freedom* (PARKETT Publishers: Zurich-Frankfurt-New York, and The MIT Press: Cambridge, Mass., 1989), p. 39.

22. Lisa Liebmann, "Progress of the Enigma," in Curiger, *op. cit.,* p. 128.

23. Nancy Spector, "Neither Bachelors Nor Brides: The Hybrid Machines of Rebecca Horn," in *Rebecca Horn* (exhibition catalogue, the Solomon R. Guggenheim Foundation: New York, 1993), p. 63.

24. Spector, *Ibid.*

25. Curiger, *op. cit.,* pp. 130-31.

26. Barbara Haskell and John G. Hanhardt, *Yoko Ono: Arias and Objects* (Peregrine Smith Books: Salt Lake City, 1991), p. 100.

27. Kristine McKenna, "Yoko Reconsidered," *Los Angeles Times/Calendar,* April 11, 1993, p. 80.

28. McKenna, *op. cit.,* p. 81.

29. Mckenna, *op. cit.,* p. 80.

30. Yoko Ono, *Grapefruit* (Simon and Schuster:New York, 1970), unpaginated.

31. Both in Ono, *op. cit..*

32. Haskell, *op. cit.,* p. 91.

33. Mckenna, *op. cit.,* p. 80.

34. *Ibid.*

35. "Witchcraft offers the model of a religion of poetry, not theology. It presents metaphors, not doctrines, and leaves open the possiblity of reconciliation...of many ways of knowing. It functions in those deeper ways of knowing which our culture has denied and for which we hunger. The world view of Witchcraft is cyclical, spiral. It dissolves dualities and sees opposites as complements." Miriam Samos (aka Starhawk), quoted in Michael Tucker, *Dreaming With Open Eyes: The Shamanic Spirit in Twentieth Century Art and Culture* (Aquarian/Harper: San Fransisco, 1992), p. 197.

36. Deborah Wye, *Louise Bourgeois* (exhibition catalogue, The Museum of Modern Art: New York, 1983), p. 23.

37. See note 36.

38. Eleanor Flomenhaft, "Interviewing Faith Ringgold/A Contemporary Heroine," in Eleanor Flomenhaft, *Faith Ringgold: A 25 Year Survey* (exhibition catalogue, Fine Arts Museum of Long Island,: Hempstead, N.Y., 1990).

39. "Faith Ringgold," in Eleanor Munro, *Originals: American Women Artists* (Simon and Schuster: New York, 1979), p. 414.

40. Thalia Gouma-Peterson, " Modern Dilemna Tales: Faith Ringgold's Story Quilts," in Flomenhaft, *op. cit.,* p. 23.

41. *Ibid.*

42. *Ibid.*

43. Roberta Smith, "Quilted Narratives," *New York Times*, February 14, 1992.

44. Lisa Phillips, " Cindy Sherman's Cindy Shermans," in *Cindy Sherman* (exhibition catalogue, Whitney Museum of American Art: New York, 1987), p. 15.

45. Phillips, *op. cit.,* p. 14.

THEY DIE 8 YEARS SOONER.

THEY ARE MORE LIKELY TO BE HOMELESS THAN ANY OTHER GROUP.

PARTS OF THEIR SEX ORGANS ARE AMPUTATED AT BIRTH.

THEY HAVE TO EXPOSE THEIR BREASTS IN PUBLIC.

THEY ARE NOT ALLOWED TO EXPRESS THEIR EMOTIONS.

WHO ARE THEY?

Erika Rothenberg
Men, 1993 (detail)

YOU'RE LESS APT TO BE A BAD GIRL IF:

YOU'RE REASONABLY SURE YOU COULD SURVIVE IN THE SUBURBS WITHOUT TAKING PROZAC.

YOU THINK WRIST CORSAGES MAKE SENSE.

IF THEY'D AGREE TO IT, YOU'D PICK TIPPER AND AL AS GODPARENTS TO YOUR KIDS.

YOU'VE LEARNED EVERYTHING YOU KNOW ABOUT VIOLENCE FROM NETWORK TELEVISION.

YOU IDENTIFY MORE WITH SANDRA DEE THAN SANDRA BERNHARD.

YOU'VE NEVER PEED IN A SWIMMING POOL OR LIED IN A PERSONAL AD.

YOU'RE MORE APT TO BE A BAD GIRL IF:

THE FIRST THING TO CROSS YOUR MIND AFTER GETTING AN INVITATION TO THE WHITE HOUSE IS, "WHERE DID I PUT MY WOOPIE CUSHION?"

THE PROSPECT OF GETTING A MARRIAGE PROPOSAL FROM ROSEANNE AND TOM ARNOLD ISN'T AT ALL REPUGNANT.

YOU DON'T KEEP YOUR CRISCO IN THE KITCHEN.

YOU FEEL CLOSER TO LINDA ELLERBEE THAN YOU EVER COULD TO DIANE SAWYER.

YOUR VIBRATOR IS USED MORE THAN YOUR ELECTRIC CAN OPENER.

SOMEONE MADE YOUR HAIR A PRIMARY COLOR AND YOU DIDN'T SUE.

Sybil Sage
Wall Texts, 1994

Ann Agee
Lake Michigan Bathroom, 1992

Lynda Benglis
advertisement, *Artforum* 13
(November 1974)

Coreen Simpson
Untitled, 1980

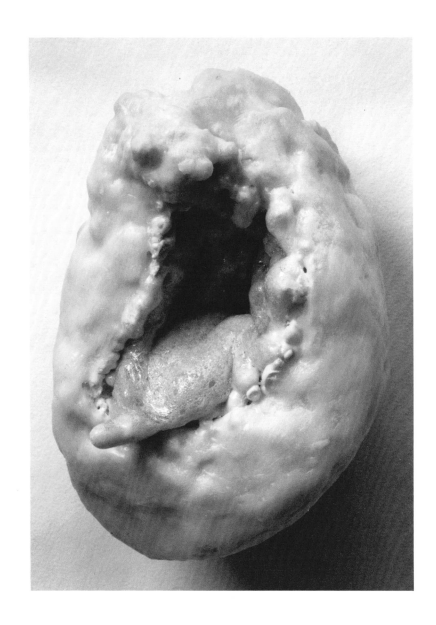

Maxine Hayt
Lick #1, 1993

Portia Munson
Pink Project, 1994

Rona Pondick
Plums, 1993

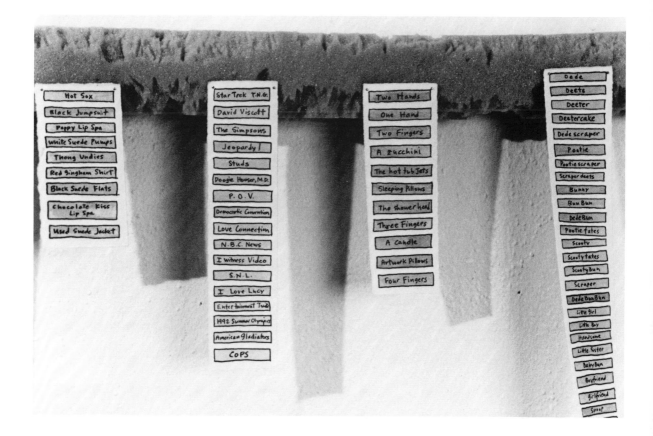

Anne Walsh
Legend, 1992-93 (detail)

Janine Antoni
Mom and Dad, 1993

Nancy Davidson
Overly Natural, 1993

Barbara Brandon
I'm Going to Keep My Father's Name,
1993

Jennifer Camper
Heterosexuals in the Military, 1993

Elaine Tin Nyo
Untitled (Gorzynski Portfolio), 1992

Gaza Bowen
Shoes for the Little Woman, 1986

Keith Boadwee
Jasmine Swami, 1993

"All That She Wants": Transgressions, Appropriations, and Art

Linda Goode Bryant

Lack of brain, nor wit, nor sturdy brawn will lead to a woman's peril.
T'is the shame she bears from the weight of stares
that befall a clumsy girl!

Charm.

We stood. Catty-corner in an open circle, elbows tight, nose up, chin forward, smile. "Not too wide."

She cautioned.

Heel to ball of foot, toe. Walk. Heel to ball of foot, toe. Repeat. Heel to ball of foot. Toe.

"That's right. You two, to the center. Very nice. Next."

We were. Ducklings. Gliding imperceptibly from the front to the back of a soft cushioned couch. We could unbutton, effortlessly, the pearl of a white fitted glove while our hands lay poised on laps with legs that crossed at the ankles.

"Light of foot, full of grace, balance, poise and an angel's face."

School.

Within moments we would be Swans, Ducklings who had crossed the circle. And, with a book balanced high upon the head, we would greet our partners, curtsy with a tilt and then turn with a smile that flirted along lips which curled and threatened to pout.
We. With each thought measured and each measure learned, we were always eager, willing, and prepared.

**And we shared and we would share only the things that
Ducklings share once they are Swans.**

Then.

**It fell. I grabbed for it, but it had slipped from my head and hit my shoul-
der, fell through my hands and cut the circle, skirting the floor with its
pages torn and its covers bent.**

I tried.

**I closed my eyes and I tried. But. It would not go away. It just lay there,
atop her foot, having snagged the leg of her flesh colored stockings.**

"It left a nasty bruise."

She told the mothers.

**So I stood among moments out of time listening to the body for its soul.
But in a circle made with folded arms, only the others whispered.**

A nearly all-white rural school in Morocco, Ind., has been rife with tension over white girls wearing baggy clothes, braids and other so-called
black fashions.

Since mid-November, at least five girls have withdrawn from North
Newton Junior-Senior High after being jeered and spit on by boys
accusing them of "acting black."[1]

The *Bad Girls* and *Bad Girls West* exhibitions bring together artists whose
works have been identified as *transgressive*—works which speak to a female
identity that exists outside conventional feminine traits, aspirations and decorum. Inclusive by design, *Bad Girls* centers on work which is often outrageous and funny, provocative and irreverent.

But what does it take to be a "bad girl" today, when so much of contemporary
western imagery and language is appropriated from the cultures of others? Is
it possible to construct valid personal or political identities from cultural frag-
ments or from an affinity to another's experience? And if so, what are the
political and social ramifications of such a construction?
Bad Girls offers a unique opportunity for the viewer to look at cultural appro-

priation in relation to work being created—largely by women—which seeks to (re)define and (re)position the female in contemporary society. Are we "bad" or are we simply following conventional suit in a process that may in fact undermine our very intent?[2]

Art, politics, and the public make curious relations. Both bound and estranged by their vested interests, they merge and reemerge into fluid forums that shape and define the context of culture. Conspirators and adversaries whose allegiances constantly shift as they jockey amongst themselves for position and influence, they are the scale, always in precarious balance, upon which society measures, confronts and makes change within itself.

Art is the moral arbiter of this trinity, or so it has come to be believed. Through its voice and vision, art is the "pure" agent, providing insight and bearing witness to the deeds and ethics of society, presumably without compromise, manipulation, or deceit.

However, when art explicitly and directly responds to prevailing social conditions, its function and sphere of influence take on added dimensions. The role of the artist changes as his/her public, political and artistic voices are elevated and merged into a single voice, each part having equal import and measure. Think about Madonna, Chuck D, Spike Lee, Wynton Marsalis, Susan Sarandon, Ron Silver, Bill T. Jones, Jenny Holtzer, Barbara Kruger, Adrian Piper, John Ahearn, Tim Rollins & KOS, and Barbara Streisand. To varying degrees in the public's perception and expectation, they have transcended their "role" as artists. No longer are they just artists; they have become political leaders or public advocates who speak from the vantage point of art's insight and moral status, which inform their thoughts, words and actions.

Recast with political and public authority, art's social influence—and that of its makers—increases exponentially. Subsequently, it would seem, artists' responsibility and accountability to society increase in order to ensure that the "insight" and "moral" functions of art are not compromised or undermined for political expediency, personal gain, or public favor.

Fulfilling this obligation, however, is complicated if artmakers rely upon appropriated cultural forms for their inspiration and expression. In such instances, the artist is a predator in a process that culturally and socially dis-

Renée Cox
Mother and Child, 1993

enfranchises appropriated groups. And the art becomes the vehicle through which historical social and political inequalities are reinforced.

For instance, the international pop music star Paul Simon provided an opportunity for Black South African musicians to work and—particularly in the case of Ladysmith Black Mambazo—to perform and have their music heard worldwide. But, at the end of the "collaboration" between these musicians and Simon, it was Simon who was the sole owner of the product. Ironically, the resulting inequity in ownership was buried in the trappings of liberation and interracial harmony.

By whom and by what means culture is controlled directly affects the ways we perceive, define and function with(in) and among ourselves. Through appropriation the appropriator seizes control of another's culture. Says ethnomusicologist Stephen Feld:

> Musical appropriation sings a double line with one voice. It is a melody of admiration, even homage and respect; a fundamental source of connectedness, creativity, and innovation. This we locate in a discourse of "roots," of reproducing and expanding "the tradition." Yet this voice is harmonized by a counter-melody of power, even control and domination; a fundamental source of maintaining asymmetries in ownership and commodification of musical works. This we locate in a discourse of "rip-offs," of reproducing "the hegemonic." Appropriation means that the issue of "whose music?" is submerged, supplanted, and subverted by the assertion of "our music."[3]

Appropriation means an unequal exchange between parties, no more, no less. It is the process by which one party benefits to the detriment of the other. In cultural terms, it occurs when a community's symbols, language, beliefs, lifestyle, foodways, music, dance, art and/or traditions are taken, reinterpreted, documented, preserved, redesignated, reproduced or disseminated by and to the disproportionate benefit of those outside that community.

The example of Paul Simon is only the latest in a practice dating back to at least Irving Berlin, in the 1920s, who, according to a contemporary newspaper account, borrowed "lilts from the chants of the country Negroes of the South. Any ordinary man about town may discover that the pure source of a good deal of what will make this year's musical comedies slightly different from those of last year is the town Negro, the rhapsodic flat-dweller of the upper reaches of Harlem."[4]

The tradition extends even further back to nineteenth-century minstrel shows which, according to scholar Helga Rogers, originated as follows:

> In 1830, Thomas Rice saw a Negro boy on a Cincinnati street, singing and shouting as he danced, "Jump, Jim Crow." Rice, struck by its possibilities, copied him, blackened his face, took it on the stage and won fame and fortune.[5]

But as Rogers points out, there is evidence that blackening of the face by white entertainers occurred before the European discovery of America. For example, in performing the morris (i.e. Moorish) dance, which had its origins in Africa, Europeans blackened their faces. This dance would become known as one of the national dances of England.[6]

When a community's culture is appropriated, it loses the history that confirms and the context that inspires its being. Disassociated and displaced without sufficient or accurate reference, the community suffers the erosion of its identity and the means for its self-sufficiency, its development and growth. Reliant upon the resources of others, it becomes powerless.

Unlike the process of assimilation, the process of appropriation involves the taking by others of an indigenous form, the redesignation of the form's ownership, and the production and distribution of the transmogrified form outside and beyond the indigenous community, by others. Assimilation, on the other hand, involves a community's "giving up" its original culture in exchange for that of another. In America, the tradeoff of this forfeiture for white immigrant groups which could and can ethnically dissolve has been access to the opportunities and resources enjoyed by the privileged group, the racially assimilated population.

Insidious and ethereal by nature, the dissemination of appropriated forms through media makes the process of appropriation almost invisible to the untrained ear and eye. The dangerous repercussions of this process are intensified when the public overrelies on commercial media for information and when "speech acts" are used routinely to create a history which has no basis in fact.[7]

Speech acts confound and manipulate conventional logic by making it difficult to differentiate between language that "describes" and language that "performs." Thus they break down the distinctions between fact and fiction. Through speech acts, appropriation occurs virtually without notice and the

Perhaps native culture needs to be placed on the endangered species list along with our animals and plant relatives and be protected against destruction, exploitation, and assimilation.

How can our ceremonies, our religious rituals, be protected when sweat lodges, pipe ceremonies, or cornhusk dolls wearing false face masks are as readily accessible as K-Mart specials? Or when elements of native cultures are taken out of context and sold as objects of curiosity?

Trudie Lamb Richmond, "K-Mart's Weekend Special Indian Spirituality," *The Eagle*, Vol. II #2 Spring, 1993, as reprinted in *American Indian Community House Community Bulletin Winter*, 1993, p.9.

depradation of appropriation comes about with no apparent cause, enabling the appropriator to operate without guilt and often unknowingly; worse, the appropriated themselves, unaware, unwittingly participate in the mining of their resources to the benefit of others.

Alice Walker, the Pulitzer Prize-winning novelist, is a current example of how someone can appropriate presumably without intent. In her documentary film and non-fiction book *Warrior Marks*, 1993, Walker purports to expose and fight what she defines as female genital mutilation—a practice which involves the circumcision, excision, or infibulation of external female genitalia. Still prevalent in parts of Africa and Asia and among immigrant communities in Western Europe and North America, this practice is a rite of passage for females.

During childhood, Walker was accidentally blinded in one eye by her brother; in her presentation, she likens this event to the cultural practice of female genital mutilation. By drawing such an affinity, she positions herself among and equal in experience to those women who have undergone circumcision. She essentially appropriates their experience in order to claim inclusion in their group, an inclusion which allows her to speak for them. Unfortunately, when she speaks, Walker becomes a type of feminist postmodern imperialist, who portrays

> an African village where women and chidren are without personality, dancing and gazing blankly through some stranger's script of their lives. The respected elder women of the village's Secret Society turn into slit-eyed murderers wielding rusted weapons with which to butcher children.
>
> As is common in Western depictions of Africa, Walker...portray[s] the continent as a monolith. African women and children are the props, and the village the background against which Alice Walker, heroine-savior, comes to articulate their pain and condemn those who inflict it.[8]

Forms are usually appropriated for art because of their uniqueness within the context of the *larger* society. As such, these forms instantly give art the appearance of originality without making creative requirements of its maker. To ensure conceptual ownership and acknowledgment, the artist alters, obscures, or denies the form's origins and original context. This s/he accomplishes by "referencing," that is, omission (extracting the appropriated form and presenting it as original), juxtaposition (defining art by its relative position to the form), or association (implying that similar circumstance exists between the art and the form). Referencing gives a work of art its identity, endows it with meaning, validates its significance, and enhances its position artistically and historically. Conversely, referencing makes the form subordinate to the art it has endowed by stripping the form of its original content and meaning.

Basically, there are three types of referencing: cultural, racial, and sexual. Cultural referencing is most often used in (re)designating a given form and (re)interpreting its meaning. This type of referencing is frequently used by institutions and is informed by their cultural bias. For example, in his critique of the Museum of Modern Art exhibition *"Primitivism" in 20th Century Art: Affinity of the Tribal and the Modern*, James Clifford identifies and analyzes evidence of this type of bias:

> Nowhere...does the exhibition or catalogue underline a more disquieting quality of modernism; its taste for appropriating or redeeming otherness, for constituting non-Western arts in its own image, for discovering universal, ahistorical "human" capacities.... Indeed an ignorance of cultural context seems almost a precondition for artistic appreciation. In this object system a tribal piece is detached from one milieu in order to circulate freely in another, a world of art—of museums, markets, and connoisseurship.[9]

The inaccuracies and distortions that result from cultural referencing are also evident in the display and interpretation of contemporary art when the ethnicity and culture of the artist are different from those of the scholar or cultural institution. A classic instance is provided in the description on a wall label for a work exhibited in a recent museum exhibition: "David Hammons' *Untitled* sculpture of 1992, for example, with black hair clippings reminiscent of dread locks, compels *viewers* to recognize their phobic responses to bodily signs of difference."[10]

Racial referencing is a common tactic used to legitimize or ascribe qualities to art (and to artists) that do not actually exist. When this type of referencing is used in conjunction with a speech act, it can indicate the performance of an action that never occured. Thus it is, for example, that the actor Sylvester Stallone has been credited as the man responsible for the word "Yo," when the fact is that Stallone, or those who wrote his scripts, simply appropriated

Very good, used esp. in emphatic form, baad. Cf. Michael Jackson's "I'm baad!" Similar are *mean,* in sense of satisfying, fine, attractive; *wicked,* in sense of excellent, capable. Cf. African use of negative terms, pronounced emphatically, to describe positive extremes: Mandingo (Bambara) *a ka Nyi Ko-jigi,* it's very good! (lit. "it is good badly!"); Mandingo (Gambia) *a nyinata jag-ke,* she is very beautiful! Also West African English (Sierra Leone) *gud baad,* it's very good!

Joseph E. Holloway and Winifred K. Vass, *The African Heritage of American English,* (Indiana University Press: Bloomington, 1993), p. 137.

the word from its urban use by African-Americans and Latinos. In the process, Stallone has become for millions of people creative, "original," and "hip," which has certainly has not hurt his box office potential. Sylvester Stallone, like Paul Simon, it should be noted, is a financial winner in the film, television and record industry, which happens to be America's second largest export, yielding $3.79 billion annually.[11]

Which brings us to the use of the word "bad" in the title of this exhibition, *Bad Girls.* Here is an example of how racial referencing occurs long after an appropriated word has gone into the "public domain."

It is commonly believed that the word "bad" (meaning good) has its origins in African-American English. As used by African-Americans "bad" denotes its opposite meaning in American English. This use has been designated by recent intellectual and political discourse as a deliberately "transgressive" act, a defiant response to political and social oppression. Thus, the use and application of the word "bad" in American English has come to denote transgression, endowing the speaker or the subject it describes with qualities associated with African-Americans. Therefore, the assimilated population—the racial other of African-Americans—can become "hip," "unique" and "original" through referencing, without genuine effort and without "transgressive" or "political" action.

Moreover, research has shown that the use of "bad" as good has African origins.[12] Winifred Vass and Joseph Holloway in *The African Heritage of American English*, in addition to identifying Bantu vocabulary in Gullah and African-American English, have detected over 200 words and Africanisms in contemporary American English, including "bad," "chick" as in beautiful girl (Wolof), "bowdacious" (Bantu), "guy" (Wolof), "hulla ballo," (Mandingo), "okay" (Mandingo), "uh-huh" (widespread African usage), and "rap" (Sierra Leone).[13]

Many of these words are no longer acknowledged as having African or African-American origins. Those that do—"jazz" (Bantu), "jive" (Wolof), and "skin" as in "give me some skin" (Mandingo)—are commonly used to attribute qualities, experiences, and actions to the assimilated group simply through word association.

Historically, racial referencing has been used as a short-cut to defining oneself in terms of the "other." A highly praised film from New Zealand, Jane

Campion's *The Piano*, is a classic example of how this device works. Through Campion's negative portrayal of indigenous people in juxtaposition to European colonizers, the white characters in this film become flesh and bone, "real." Not only does this referencing give the European characters substance, but when juxtaposed with the natives—portrayed as void of culture and dignity—it makes them both prominent and superior, and it gives definition to their "cultural" ethics and morality. Through negative portraits of indigenous people, Campion gives her protagonist and fellow Europeans definition and a context and rationale for their behavior.

Thus, the artistic necessity of defining and developing characters, places, forms, and events has been expeditiously collapsed by many artists into the simple and far too easy process of appropriation.

Gender or sexual referencing, like racial referencing, can be used as a short cut in assigning actions, meanings, and characteristics to a speaker or subject that otherwise do not exist. For instance, in hip-hop culture the term "bitch" is shorthand for undesirable *female* traits or actions by men as well as women. Unlike the use of racial referencing to endow one group with qualities and experiences in contrast to another, gender referencing is more commonly used to show differences between males and females. By stripping one sex (usually female) of admirable qualities, the qualities of the opposite are enhanced.

Perhaps the most peculiar and most damaging fallout from such referencing in contemporary art and popular culture is the impact that improper or inaccurate references have. This occurs when the artist appropriates the indigenous form without knowledge or understanding, and uses it out of context.

"All That She Wants" is a current popular song by a European pop group, "Ace of Base." With a "rap" inspired name and a reggae beat, this song tells the story of a woman who hunts men so she can have "another baby." What the story fails to convey is whether the "baby" is child or lover. This confusion is probably unintentional, the result of the misappropriation of "American" popular language. At best, the song makes little or no sense.

Though they seem benign, the lyrics of "All That She Wants" are anti-female. Sung by women, the song portrays its protagonist as a "hunter," an unconventional woman who aggressively seeks relationships on her own. However, if this independence is meant to be "bad," i.e., good, then the song's improper

Proprietors of employment agencies are being importuned to supply cooks, waitresses, laundresses and maids "who can Charleston." Women who employ Negro servants adept in the combination wing and step are implored by friends to obtain for them servants similarly skilled. The domestic helper who works by day and "sleeps in" need offer no excuses for tasks incompleted if they can show their employers how to do a passable Charleston. The visiting laundress will hear no complaint about her slowness if she can "shake a leg." Burned food, late luncheon or dinner, dust in the corners of the remains of Sunday's ham intended for Monday consumption are forgiven if the offender can only impart to her mistress that elusive winging movement of the legs without which there is no authentic Charleston.

"Charleston A Hit in Home, Dance Hall and Ballroom," *New York Times*, May 24, 1925, quoted in *Harlem on My Mind*, ed. Allon Schoener (Dell Publishing Co. Inc.: New York, 1968), p. 66.

contextualization of American slang makes her more viper than feminist. If, on the other hand, the song has her hunting men purely for the purpose of procreation, she is no less a viper for it. Either way, the juxtaposition of independent woman with viper undermines the substance of female independence and self-determination, to say nothing of portraying women, whether conventional or progressive, as treacherous.

Gender referencing for identity also occurs in Jane Campion's *The Piano*, which provides a less than loving portrayal of a woman who seems, on the surface, to be affectionately and sympathetically portrayed. But while the female protagonist is presented as self-determining—and thus, within the film's context, independent, a feminist of sorts—the references Campion uses to define her are male and her actions are only rational if seen from a male perspective. How otherwise could it be explained that she, in fact, falls in love with the man for whom she is a whore and for whom she gives up her own distinct "voice" in order to conform with his? This so-called romantic tale reinforces oppressive gender stereotypes while giving the appearance of liberation.

If one's identity is defined by referencing its "other"—especially if that other has historically participated in one's oppression—then it is that other who retains power and control over identity and action. This occurs in spite of the hype, the style, and the image presented by the "formerly" oppressed.

So it is that young African-American women and girls have come to embrace negative female descriptions and images to define themselves as independent and "bad." Be it rap artist MC Lyte, who wants a "RuffNeck," or slogans on popular sweatshirts like "I'm a Gangster Bitch," the reference, the style, and the attitude are male. And, my sistahs, referencing a male in order to define yourself, no mattah how bad you be—as opposed to referencing your female self to define woman—well, that maintains the status quo. And it strengthens and reinforces the gender hierarchy. In this situation, women are no longer "mere" objects of oppression but also accomplices in their own subjugation. So how "bad," darlin', do you really be?

In an environment where individuals lack the tools for active research, investigation and critical analysis, when words supported by images become "acts" that are the basis upon which we make decisions, and when referencing others is the means by which we define ourselves, art must be especially vigiliant. It must be open to examination and reexamination of its influences and be clear in its meaning and intent. It must above all be self-critical.

If art is to fulfill its responsibility within the trinity of art, politics and the public, it will deconstruct the process of appropriation, expose "speech acts," and become a catalyst and inspiration for critical thought and analysis.

To sum up: in its most fundamental application, appropriation provides the appropriator with the means to claim something which s/he has not done, to experience something which s/he has not experienced, to assume responsibility for something for which s/he has no charge. Appropriation provides the *appearance* of something without the action or event. Through its lens, it is the spectacle of leadership and not its evidence, the idea of culture and not its experience that shapes and informs the art.

And the "bad girls?" Well, those are the good ones—those who find agency through self and not through the appropriation of the cultural forms of others. Bad girls make art that comes out of experience and not style, out of conviction, not trend; they reference themselves, not others. Bad girls are those who, in a circle made with folded arms, can stand alone and hear their souls.

It is this writer's hope that viewers will look at *Bad Girls* and *Bad Girls West* in a spirit of inquiry that goes *inside* the concept of "transgression" and *under* art's image and style. What, in fact, they will ask themselves, is its substance and content? What is the *meaning* of its politics?

1. "Students Spurn 'Black Fashion,'" *New York Newsday*, December 8, 1993.

2. The concepts of cultural appropriation discussed in this paper were developed with intellectual support and research provided by Howard Weiss, challenged and revised through conversations with Brienin and Kenneth Bryant, and supported with information supplied by Paul Goode and Susan Tucker.

3. Steven Feld, "Notes on World Beat," *Public Culture Bulletin*, Vol. 1, No. 1, Fall 1988, p. 31.

4. James Whittaker, "Irving Berlin Borrowed Chants from South," *Sunday News*, May 8, 1921, quoted in *Harlem on My Mind*, ed. Allon Schoener (Dell Publishing Co., Inc.: New York, 1968), p. 53.

5. Helga M. Rogers, *Africa's Gift to America* (Helga M. Rogers: New York, 1961), p. 232.

6. See *Ibid*, p. 237.

7. "Speech act" has been defined by J.L. Austin as "...that kind of speech [which] rather than stating something, actually does something." See Claudia Brodsky Lacour, "Doing Things With Words: 'Racism' as Speech Act and the Undoing of Justice," in *Race-ing Justice, En-gendering Power*, ed. Toni Morrison (Pantheon Books: New York, 1992), p. 134. Lacour in her essay analyzes Clarence Thomas's use of speech acts to deflect the allegations of sexual harrassment made against him by Anita Hill.

8. Seble Dawit and Salem Mekuria, "The West Just Doesn't Get It," *New York Times*, December 7, 1993.

9. James Clifford, *The Predicament of Culture: Twentieth-Century Ethnography, Literature, and Art* (Harvard University Press: Cambridge, Mass., 1988), p. 193.

10. *Abject Art,* Whitney Museum of Art, New York, 1993. (Emphasis added.)

11. See "Culture Dispute with Paris Now Snags World Accord," *New York Times*, December 8, 1993.

12. Lorenzo Dow Turner, in *Africanisms in the Gullah Dialect* (Chicago: University of Chicago Press, 1949), was the first to provide significant evidence that Africans in America had retained Africanisms, notably Bantu. Turner's research has been expanded in Joseph E. Holloway and Winifred K. Vass, *The African Heritage of American English* (Indiana University Press: Bloomington, 1993), see pp. ix-xi.

13. See Holloway and Vass, *op. cit.*, passim.

Possessed

Cheryl Dunye

Bad Girls

Over the past few months I've been approached by every woman video artist I know and asked the question "What's this *Bad Girls* show all about?" My responses have ranged from "Postmodern feminist production" to a long-winded answer which usually takes several hours and a few drinks. But when asked to write about it I find myself stymied as to what to say. The questions raised in this show leave me wondering what being an artist, a "bad girl" artist, is all about. Is it being sexually explicit in one's work or being transgressive and political in one's work? Although in general the included works are a response to these questions, they share one even more transgressive feature: humor. Though never really specified, humor appears in every video included in this show. *Bad Girls* intends explicitly to address recent video production that has a sense of humor when discussing issues in the broad terrain of feminist politics. And with this very open definition in hand, I want to discuss my personal understandings of the term "bad girl" and some of my opinions on "bad girlism" as it relates to this exhibition.

Bad Girl

In recent years I feel more like good girl than a bad girl. In the early 1980s, after realizing what my dark skin really meant to my white schoolmates and what my "white girl" values really meant to my black schoolmates and most importantly what my not-so-straight "desire" for several girl schoolmates meant to me, I decided that I was a lesbian. And not your simple "I-love-another-woman" lesbian, but an anarcho-lesbian feminist separatist—a bad girl. Three days after my high school graduation I "came out" loud and strong, cutting my straightened permed hair into a Mr. T Mohawk, wearing combat

Lee Williams/Angela Anderson
Love, Boys and Food, 1993 (video still)

boots and ripped thrift store clothing, and of course, the single earlobe filled
with many anarchist, lesbian, and feminist symbols of rebellion—a *bad* girl.
And you know what? I loved it. I loved being a part of a group (at the time a
very small white group) of "wimmin" who wanted to smash the state, end
patriarchy, and love one another openly— a bad girl. For me a bad girl meant
being different, different from who I was or who I was supposed to become.
A bad girl meant being other, other from who I was and other from the
"other" I would soon realize I was.

By 1985, the term black was missing from my life so I tried to add it to my
anarcho-lesbian feminist separatist label. This of course didn't go over well
with the white girls in the gang, so I became a self-actualized Afrocentric lesbian street vendor of jewelry made only by other self-actualized Afrocentric
lesbian street vendors. I would walk through the early morning rush hour
traffic with my table and wares, setting up across from an office building
where secretaries did lunch time shopping for earrings and spirituality. They
would ask about my dreadlocks. "Why do you wear you hair like that?
Doesn't it mean you are a Rastafarian?"

"No," I'd respond, "I am a self-actualized Afrocentric woman working outside of the system to create networks which empower other women like
myself"—a bad girl.

Diane Bonder
Dangerous When Wet, 1992 (video still)

And this time I was a bad girl not because of my race but because of my sexual preference. When confronted by a male Afrocentric vendor, I would lie. Not out of fear mind you, but out of the need to be connected to an empowered community which, in the long run, I never became a part of.

Which brings me to the 1990s and my schizophrenic feelings about identity and politics. I was tired of being black when everyone else was white and being lesbian when everyone else was straight. So instead of becoming something else, I decided to check out something my parents always wanted me to be—a *good* girl. A good girl truthfully talks about who she is and how she feels. So in 1990 me and my good-girl self pick up a video camera and humorously tell the world my life in a video entitled *Janine.* In the video I talk about my racial and class differences with a girl I had a crush on in high school. I also reveal how these differences and my desire for her shaped who I am today: black, woman, and lesbian at the same time. Now I'm a good girl who is good, bad, and everything. But is this a bad girl being good or a good girl being bad???

Bad Girls

In the politically correct world of feminist video production, humor tends to clash with things like sexism, racism, and oppression. You generally don't find many women-of-color artists poking fun at their race and you *especially* won't find any white women who would attempt to make any jokes about the issue. There seems to be something too provocative and painful in humor that crosses these personal and political lines— something a bit incorrect (remember the Whoopi Goldberg and Ted Danson incident at the Friars Club?). Lately I wonder about these notions of correctness and question their "correctness." Why can't women talk about serious personal and political things in an unserious fashion? Are women artists afraid that humor might weaken the intensity of the issue at hand? I don't know the answer, but recently I've seen several videos by some women artists who do know. With video camera in hand and little funds in their pockets, a new wave of women video artists have created their own definition for correctness, producing works that are smart, political and, most important, funny. They are the *Bad Girl* video artists included in this show. In their works they actively arrange materials in such a manner that almost anyone can enter into, participate with laughter, and then step back to examine the sometimes personal sometimes political issues and one's relationship to them.

In gathering videos for this show, I was surprised to have received many, many videos from lesbians, a few from sex activists and men, and almost none from women of color. Confused, I began a search for works by women of color that were both humorous and transgressive. There were numerous listings of them in all of the distribution catalogues, but none seem to fit the qualifications for this particular show. I began wondering if there is something about "bad girlism" that excludes discussions of race, because most women-of-color video artists tend to make work about their community, class, and spirituality. Rather than poking fun at these issues, I think these women artists find it more important to bring them into existence, and therefore few videos by them appear in this show.

Bad Girl

Now that I've labeled my self a "good girl" video artist, I'm beginning to wonder if I'm still a bad girl. As a black lesbian artist, I am constantly making fun of lesbian issues, making jokes about being a woman— and poking fun about being black. To many this form of art making doesn't do much for the socio-political revolution we've all been waiting for, or does it? To date, I've produced four videos and have made over 4,000 people laugh; not only black lesbians but all kinds of people. I think my irreverent use of humor allows viewers to focus on the bigger picture of how the presented materials are intertwined in our lives: we are all connected. For me being a video artist means creating spaces where humans—black, white, male, female— communicate. And if this is what being a bad girl is all about then ... call me a *Bad Girl.*

Bad Girls Checklist

The New Museum
of Contemporary Art

All works are courtesy of the artist
unless otherwise noted.

Ann Agee

Lake Michigan Bathroom, 1992
Porcelain; 108 x 132"

Laura Aguilar

Untitled Self Portrait, 1991
Gelatin silver print; 50 x 40"
Self Portrait, 1993
Gelatin silver print; 16 x 20"

Gwen Akin/Allan Ludwig

The Women Series, 1992
Installation with 200 gelatin
silver prints
Courtesy Pamela Auchincloss Gallery,
New York

Janine Antoni

Mom and Dad, 1993
Mother, Father, makeup; 24 x 20"
Courtesy Sandra Gehring Gallery,
New York

Xenobia Bailey

Sistah Paradise's Revival Tent, 1993
Installation, mixed media;
Dimensions variable

Lillian Ball

Phobots Series, 1993
Rubber, electronics; 24 dildos,
10 x 4 x 4" each
Hand Job, 1993
Rubber, battery, motors, steel;
10 dildos, 9 x 72 x 10" each

Lynda Barry

A Sandwich, 1984
Watercolor on paper; 12 x 15"
All Day, 1993
Ink on paper; 2 panels, 7 x 11" each
Fury, 1993
Ink on paper; 2 panels, 7 x 11" each
God's Gift, 1985
Watercolor on paper; 15 x 20"
Little String, 1993
Ink on paper; 2 panels, 7 x 11" each

Elizabeth Berdann

10 of My Best Facial Features, 1993
Oil on copper, engraved brass, found
objects; 25 x 30"
Courtesy Josh Baer Gallery, New York
Topless Hall of Fame, 1993
Oil on copper, engraved copper;
144 x 204"
Courtesy Josh Baer Gallery, New York
Rocket, 1993
Oil on copper; 120 x 96"
Courtesy Josh Baer Gallery, New York

Camille Billops

Minstrel Series, 1992
Gold, pencil on arches;
8 panels, 22 x 30" each

Molly Bleiden

Transparent Image Design Studio:
The Desk of Visual Splendor, 1993
Installation with plexiglas, telephones,
motorized chair, six channels of
audio, printed material, filing cabinet;
132 x 144"

Keith Boadwee

Homer Swami, 1993
Duraflex print; 48 x 60"
Collection Tom Patchett, Los Angeles
Elmo Swami, 1993
Duraflex print; 60 x 48"
Courtesy Kim Light Gallery, Los
Angeles
Jasmine Swami, 1993
Duraflex print; 60 x 48"
Collection Clyde and Karen Beswick,
Los Angeles

Andrea Bowers

Indignant Fairy Weather Vane, 1993
Bronze, copper, steel; 32 x 36 x 36"
Courtesy Food House,
Santa Monica

Lisa Bowman

Untitled, 1992
700 pieces of soap, letterset, varnish;
dimensions variable

Barbara Brandon

I'm Going to Keep My
Father's Name, 1993
Ink on paper; 6 x 13"
This is Frightening, 1993
Ink on paper; 6 x 13"
Makes Me Think About Never Having
Sex Again, 1993
Ink on paper; 6 x 13"

Jennifer Camper

If Men Got Pregnant, 1992
Ink on paper; 11 x 14"
All About Mei-Ling, 1993
Ink on paper; 11 x 13¾"
Caucasian Translation, 1990
Ink on paper; 11 x 14"

**New Contingency Groups for the Gay
Pride Parade**, 1992
Ink on paper; 11 x 14"
**The Advantages of Being a
Teenage Dyke**, 1992
Ink on paper; 11 x 14"
Appliance Love, 1990
Ink on paper; 11 x 14"

Renée Cox

Mother and Child, 1993
Gelatin silver print; 99½ x 63½"

Margaret Curtis

Virgin Primer, 1992
Oil on canvas; 72 x 60"
Dong Belle, 1993
Gauche on paper; 25 x 32"
Wasp, 1993
Oil on panel; 27 x 35½"

Jeanne Dunning

Untitled with Hairs, 1992
Cibachrome mounted on plexiglas,
frame; 26 x 21"
Edition 2/3
Collection Herbert Volkmann,
Berlin, Germany; courtesy Feature,
New York
Untitled with Tongue, 1990
Laminated cibachrome, frame
Artist proof; 22 x 18"
Courtesy Feature, New York
Untitled, 1988
C-print, frame; 15 x 12"
Edition 1/1
Courtesy Feature, New York
Untitled, 1988
C-print, frame
Artist proof; 15 x 12"
Courtesy Feature, New York
Untitled, 1988
C-print, frame
Artist proof; 15 x 12"
Courtesy Feature, New York

Untitled, 1988
C-print, frame
Artist proof; 15 x 12"
Courtesy Feature, New York

Nancy Dwyer

Scent of Humor: The Laughing Chairs,
1994
Baked enamel on steel, vinyl line;
4 "h" chairs, 35 x 21 x 18" each;
4 "a" chairs, 17 x 20 x 18" each
Private Collection, courtesy Josh Baer
Gallery, New York
Scent of Humor: (F) Art Table, 1993-94
Aluminum, glass, wood;
15 x 16 ½ x 20" each
Courtesy Josh Baer Gallery, New York
**Scent of Humor: Whoopie Cushion
Cushion Stools**, 1994
Heat transfer, fabric, wood; 26 x 15"
Courtesy Josh Baer Gallery, New York
**Scent of Humor: So Funny I Forgot To
Laugh**, 1994
Self adhesive vinyl; Dimensions
variable
Courtesy Josh Baer Gallery, New York

Matt Groening/Twentieth Pictures

The Simpsons: "Marge on the Lam",
½" video, 23 min.

The Guerrilla Girls

Posters and Assorted Materials
Mixed media

Jaqueline Hayden

Figure Model Series, 1991
Gelatin silver print; 80¼ x 52"
Courtesy of the artist and Howard
Yezerski Gallery, Boston
Figure Model Series, 1992
Gelatin silver print; 72 x 52"
Courtesy of the artist and Howard
Yezerski Gallery, Boston

Maxine Hayt

Lick #1, 1993
Polyurethane foam, beeswax,
encaustic; 9½ x 6½ x 6½"
Lick #2, 1993
Polyurethane foam, beeswax,
encaustic; 10½ x 8 x 6½"
Lick #3, 1993
Polyurethane foam, beeswax, encaus-
tic; 12½ x 8 x 6"
Untitled, 1993
Polyurethane foam, fabric, sisal rope,
beeswax, encaustic; 58 x 46 x 36"
Untitled, 1993
Polyurethane foam, beeswax,
encaustic; 54 x 24 x 24"
Image Bank, 1993
Postcards, photos, paper; dimensions
variable

Janet Henry

Black Goddess , 1993
Coat rack, braided waxed nylon,
color xeroxes, clear vinyl, glass beads;
67 x 23½ x 77"

Amy Hill

Salad Dressing Bottle, 1993
Mixed media; 3½ x 7"
Goy(a), 1993
2 cans, 3¾ x 3" each
Gefilte Fish, 1993
Mixed media; 4 x 9½"
Beef Franks, 1993
Mixed media; 4 x 4¾"
Miss Fitt, 1993
C-print; 36 x 20"
The Guilt Trip, 1992
C-print; 36 x 20"

Robin Kahn

High Flying Flag, 1994
Embroidery on burlap; 64 x 48"
Courtesy S.O.S. International

Nina Kuo

Cheongsam Diet, 1992
Photo emulsion on cloth; 120 x 46"
Chinese Calendar Girl and Fans, 1993
Cibachrome, text; 24¼ x 32½"

Pat Lasch

Birthing My Husband, 1992
Plaster; 4 sculptures,
9 x 6 x 5"; 4½ x 8 x 7¼";
2@ 10 x 6 x 5"
Madonna and Child, 1993
Plaster; 18 x 13 x 6"
Roladen, 1993
Plaster; 24 x 6 x 4"

Cary Leibowitz/Candyass

House of Leibowitz, 1994
Installation, with pig dolls;
dimensions variable

Lauren Lesko

Hysteria, 1991
Hat mold, circa 1930, refinished in
gold leaf; cream-colored mohair and
velvet upholstered pedestal;
39 x 12 x 12"
Collection Eileen and Peter Norton,
Santa Monica
Furburger, 1993
Neon; 9" diameter
Courtesy of the artist and Lipton
Owens Company, New York
Hair Pie, 1993
Mixed media; 46 x 12 x 12"
Mark of the beast, 1994
(a project for the *Bad Girls*) reading
room
Monkey fur, postcards;
dimensions variable

Rhonda Lieberman

Purse Pictures, 1992
Paper, glue, glitter;
7 purses, 12 x 11" each
Courtesy Stux Gallery, New York

Mabel Maney

**The Case of the Not-So-Nice-Nurse: A
Nancy Clue Mystery**, 1991
Color xerox; 5 x 7"
**The Hardly Boys in "A Ghost in the
Closet,"** 1993
Color xerox; 5½ x 5½

Yasumasa Morimura

Portrait (Futago), 1988
C-print; 102½ x 89"
Collection Suzanne and Howard
Feldman, New York
Angels Descending Staircase, 1991
C-print; 102½ x 89"
Collection PaineWebber Group Inc.,
New York

Portia Munson

Pink Project, 1994
Table covered with pink objects;
63 x 96 x 174"

Chuck Nanney

Untitled, 1992
C-print; 70 x 40"
Courtesy Jousse Seguin Gallery, Paris
Untitled, 1992
C-print; 70 x 40"
Courtesy Jousse Seguin Gallery, Paris
Untitled, 1992
C-print
70 x 40"
Courtesy Jousse Seguin Gallery, Paris

Erika Rothenberg

Men, 1993
Mixed media installation
96 x 72 x 96"
Courtesy P.P.O.W. Gallery, New
York

Veronica Saddler

Woman in a Suitcase, 1983
C-print; 16 x 20"
Woman in Red, 1983
C-print; 16 x 20"
Woman Pulling a Rope, 1983
C-print; 16 x 20"
Afternoon Swim, 1983
C-print; 16 x 20"

Monique Safford

Untitled, 1993
Acrylic on panel; 120 x 78"
Untitled, 1993
Acrylic on panel; 27 x 36"
Untitled, 1993
Acrylic on panel; 39 x 60"

Sybil Sage

Rely. It Even Absorbs the Worry, 1993
Mixed media; 24 x 28"
Wall texts, 1994
Photostats; 10 wall texts,
20 x 24" each

Joyce Scott

Regrets, 1994
Beadwork;
25 x 10 x 10 "
Madonna, 1994
Beadwork;
25 x 25 x 10 "

Beverly Semmes

Haze, 1994
Rayon velvet; 144 x 108 x 36"
Courtesy Michael Klein Gallery,
New York
Yellow Pool, 1993
Rayon velvet, organza;
dimensions variable
Commissisioned by Southeastern
Center for Contemporary Art,
Winston-Salem, North Carolina, and
Contemporary Culture, Inc.;
Courtesy Michael Klein Inc.,
New York

Susan Silas

Thurber Carnival/Fables for Our Time,
1992
Oil, enamel, linen; 75 x 105"
Private collection; courtesy Jose
Freire Fine Art, New York

Coreen Simpson

Untitled, 1980
Gelatin silver print; 20 x 24"
Black Venus, 1980
Gelatin silver print; 20 X 24"

Cindy Smith

Turn Back the Old Clock, 1993
Mixed media, altered books
36 x 96 x 24"

Elaine Tin Nyo

Daikon Half Length, 1993
Gelatin silver print;
20 x 16"
Daikon, 1993
Gelatin silver print; 20 x 16"
Twisting Carrot, 1993
Gelatin silver print; 20 x 16"
Two Daikons, 1993
Gelatin silver print; 20 x 16"

Diagonal Three Carrots, 1993
Gelatin silver print; 20 x 16"
Carrot, 1993
Gelatin silver print; 20 x 16"

Cammie Toloui

The Pleasure Palace, 1992
Installation with slides, projector;
dimensions variable

Dani Tull

Sniff (Dingle), 1993
Watercolor on duralene; 30 x 42"
Collection Johnny Depp, Los Angeles
Bumpin Fuzzies, 1993
Watercolor on duralene; 30 x 42"
Collection Clyde and Karen Beswick,
Los Angeles
Black Sheep, 1993
Watercolor on duralene; 30 x 42"
Courtesy Kim Light Gallery,
Los Angeles
Harm Farm, 1993
Watercolor on duralene; 30 x 42"
Courtesy Kim Light Gallery,
Los Angeles

Shari Urquhart

*She said "The Toys are the Father
to the War,"* 1992-93
Wool, acrylic; 88 x 112"
"Women I, Stage 3," 1994
Wool, acrylic; 90 x 110"

Carrie Mae Weems

Bride, 1989
Mixed media installation; 25 x 21½"
Courtesy P.P.O.W. Gallery, New
York

Judith Weinperson

Blue Penis, 1990
Photocopies, ragpaper, vinyl report
covers, pushpins; 168 x 174"

Read My Pussy, 1992
Photocopies, ragpaper, vinyl report
covers, pushpins; 45½ x 57"

Sue Williams

Try To Be More Accommodating, 1991
Acrylic on canvas; 15 x 18"
Private collection, New York;
Courtesy 303 Gallery, New York

Millie Wilson

Mistress, 1993
Mixed media; 70 x 21 x 12"
Private collection, courtesy Ruth
Bloom Gallery, Santa Monica

Kids!, 1994
Drawings and stories by Althea
Bardin, Isabel Jay, Hannah Kirshner
Ruby McNeil, Eliza McClaren, Leela
Ross, Nick Ross, and others.
Comic books, collection of Arthur
Greg Sulzberger.

Bad Blues, Ballads and Boogie
Audiotape, 100 min.,
compiled by Marcia Tucker

Public Programs

Saturday Afternoon Live!
Performance/Gallery talks
at The New Museum.
Saturday, January 15, at 2 pm,
with **Penny Arcade**
Saturday, March 19, at 2 pm,
with **Frieda**
Saturday, April 2, at 2 pm,
with **Carmelita Tropicana**

Reno Roast
A tribute to Reno featuring her
psychiatrist, friends, and enemies
at The New Museum.
Tuesday, February 15, at 7 pm

Opera for the Masses
Vocal performance by
The Derivative Duo
at The New Museum.
Saturday, April 2, at 4 pm

GAG: An Evening of Bad Girls
Xtra Bad Video
Video screening and panel discussion
at The New Museum.
Thursday, February 3, at 7 pm

Program:

A Spy
Suzie Silver
1992, video, 4 min.
Courtesy Video Data Bank

24 Hours a Day
Jocelyn Taylor
1993, video, 10 min.

Frenzy
Jill Reiter
1993, Super 8mm film, 10 min.

Sex Fish
E.T., Baby, Maniac
1993, video, 6 min.

Sluts and Goddesses Video Workshop
or How To Be a Sex Goddess in 101
Easy Steps
Maria Beatty/Annie Sprinkle
1992, video excerpts

Stafford's Story
Susan Muska
1992, video, 3 min.

Our Gay Brothers
Greta Snider
1993, 16mm film, 9 min.
Courtesy of the artist and
Drift Distributions

New Freedom
Camera Obscura
1993, 16mm film, 9 min.
Courtesy of the artist and
Drift Distributions

Bad Girls West Checklist

UCLA Wight Art Gallery

All works are courtesy of the artist unless otherwise noted.

Laura Aguilar

In Sandy's Room (Self-portrait), 1991
Gelatin silver print; 16 x 20"
Untitled (Self-portraits), 1993
12 gelatin silver prints, 24 x 17" each

Ken Aptekar

Job Security, 1991
Oil on wood, sandblasted glass, bolts;
30 x 60"
Collection Kristin M. Richardson,
Buffalo, NY
How Could You Believe Me?, 1992
Oil on wood, sandblasted glass, bolts;
60 x 60"
The Klinger-Gal Collection,
New York
So You Fucked the Help, 1992
Oil on wood, sandblasted glass, bolts;
30 x 60"
The Klinger-Gal Collection,
New York

Lutz Bacher

Men In Love, 1990
32 mirrors with silk-screened text;
12 x 12" each
Collection Steven and Nancy Oliver,
and Penny Cooper and Rena
Rosenwasser, Berkeley, California;
courtesy of the artist, Pat Hearn
Gallery, New York, and Kim Light
Gallery, Los Angeles.

Feminist Movement ("Sure I'm for the feminist movement. In fact, I'm pretty good at it."), 1993
Acrylic on canvas; 44 x 36 x 2"
Courtesy of the artist, Pat Hearn
Gallery, New York, and Kim Light
Gallery, Los Angeles

Lillian Ball

Crucial Protection, 1992
Rubber, binder rings; 30 x 23 x 1"
Collection Penny and David McCall,
New York
Combination Bags, 1993
Rubber, eye hooks;
72 x 98 x 6"
Tailhook, 1993-94
Mixed media installation with cast
rubber, 36 stainless steel speculums; 6
x 2 x 9" each

Judie Bamber

But Who's Counting?, 1991
Metal and wood;
Table 17¾ x 15½ x 15½",
whip 12 x 4"
Collection Clyde and Karen Beswick,
Los Angeles
How Do You Live With Yourself?, 1991
Mixed media; 34 x 15¾ x 15"
Collection Eileen and Peter Norton,
Santa Monica
My Ass and Your Vase, 1991
Metal, fresh flowers, flower frog;
Table 17¾ x 15½ x 15½",
object 12 x 4"
Courtesy of the artist and Richard
Telles Fine Art, Los Angeles
Untitled, 1991
Glow-in-the-dark vibrator with
puzzle attached;
Table 17¾ x 15½ x 15½",
object 12 x 4"
Courtesy of the artist and Richard
Telles Fine Art, Los Angeles

How Do You Trust Someone Who Bleeds for Seven Days and Doesn't Die?, 1993
Watercolor on paper;
7 watercolors, 8 x 8" each
Collection Michael and Susan Hort,
New York
I Love You To Death #1-5, 1993
Watercolor on paper;
5 watercolors, 8½ x 11" each
Courtesy of the artist and Richard
Telles Fine Art, Los Angeles

Elizabeth Berdann

Thirty of My Worst Features, 1991
Oil on metal, brass;
31 x 42 x 1" overall
Courtesy of the artist and Josh Baer
Gallery, New York
False Selves, 1992
Oil on copper, engraved brass,
enameled frames; 11 x 42"
Collection Michael and Cari Sacks,
Chicago
Freak Show!, 1993
Oil on copper, anodized aluminum;
108 x 180"
Courtesy of the artist and Josh Baer
Gallery, New York

Gaza Bowen

Shoes for the Little Woman, 1986
Toilet brushes, sponges, dish rags,
dish mops, scrubby, scouring pads,
kidskin, dish drainer, contact paper;
14 x 22 x 16"
Courtesy Couturier Gallery,
Los Angeles
Tuff Scuffs, 1990
Detergent bottles, scrubby, sponge,
sponge cloth, scrub brush, scouring
pad, cardboard, color xerox;
22 x 15 x 8"
Courtesy Couturier Gallery,
Los Angeles

In God We Trust, 1991
Leather, $20 bills;
Shoes 4½ x 5 x 13"; briefcase
4 x 13 x 17¾"
Collection Los Angeles County
Museum of Art, Costume Council
Fund (M.90.207a-c)

Kathe Burkhart

*Fuck You: from the Liz Taylor Series
(Cleopatra)*, 1987
Acrylic on canvas; 72 x 48"
Nosduh Collection, courtesy Feature,
New York
*Slit: from the Liz Taylor Series (Ash
Wednesday)*, 1992
Acrylic and gauze on canvas; 42 x 48"

Jerome Caja

Appliances for the Damned, 1990
Lipstick, whiteout, eyeliner, nail
polish on tar paper; 11 x 10"
Looking Pretty in the Mission, 1990
Enamel on paper; 2¾ x 1¾"
The Annunciation, 1990
Nail polish on enameled tin tray;
6 x 4½"
The Castrator, 1990
Gouache, eyeliner, saline solution on
jeans label; 8 x 5¾"
Victory in the Kitchen, 1990
Enamel on paper; 3¾ x 1¾"
*Joan of Arc Being Burnt on Toasters
Because She Wouldn't Do Housework*,
1991
Enamel, eyeliner, gouache on paper;
6½ x 4½"
The Immaculate Conception, 1991
Whiteout, enamel on 1940 calendar;
13½ x 10½"
Bird Yelling at Her Eggs, 1992
Wax crayons, whiteout, eyeliner,
enamel on paper, lace; 8 x 6"
Expectant Mother Smoking, 1992
Enamel on foil paper, lace;
8¾ x 6¾"

San Francisco Drag, 1992
Nail polish on plaster; 5¾ x 4¾"
Collection Deborah Brown, St. Louis,
Missouri
The Happy Virgin in the Garden, 1992
Rhoplex, nail polish on used con-
doms, eraser, human ash (Charles);
12¼ x 7¾"
Collection Tom Patchett, Los Angeles
Virgins with Capers, 1992
Nail polish on anchovy tin, wood;
9½ x 7"
A Friend Like You, 1993
Nail polish on page of found book;
7 x 12"
Ascension of the Drag Queen, 1993
Nail polish on paper; 17 x 7½"
B: Betty in the Bear Trap (from an illus-
trated alphabet in progress),
1993
Nail polish, eyeliner, whiteout,
enamel on paper; 8½ x 6¼"
Bird Out of the Cage, 1993
Nail polish, shell, tin on wood;
9" diameter
Funeral for Jack in the Box, 1993
Gouache and watercolor on wood;
12 x 10"
Collection Tom Patchett, Los Angeles
Goldilocks and the Three Bears, 1993
Nail polish on board; 10¼ x 12"
Killer Shoes, 1993
Acrylic, eyeliner, nail polish on wood;
6¾ x 8¾"
Madam Butterfly, 1993
Nail polish, acrylic, ink, enamel, eye-
liner on tin; 9½ x 12 x 2"
*Miss Tina Having Her Cake and Eating
It Too* and *Miss Tina at Her Toilette*,
1993
Nail polish and enamel on foil,
framed in plastic dog dish; 5½ x 11"
(diptych)
Mister Sister, 1993
Gouache, nail polish, eyeliner on
wood; 7⅛ x 6⅛"
Collection Tom Patchett, Los Angeles

New Boobies, 1993
Enamel, whiteout, nail polish on
paper, lace mat; 16 x 12¾"
Spermicide, 1993
Eyeliner, acrylic ink, tempera, nail
polish on paper; 13¾ x 10½"
Stepsisters, 1993
Nail polish on metal;
2 parts, 5½ x 4¾" each
The Bearded Lady, 1993
Nail polish on metal, "pearl"
necklace; 2¾" diameter
*The Morning Goddess Making
Breakfast*, 1993
Eyeliner, acrylic ink, nail polish on
wood; 7¼ x 6¼"
The Virgin Chicken Spanking Her Eggs,
1993
Nail polish on plaster; 7½ x 5½"
Virgin at the Hamper, 1993
Nail polish on paper; 10 x 7"
Virgin Opener with Cherry, 1993
Nail polish, ceramic, plastic;
4¾ x 3¼"
Which One Doesn't Belong? 1993
Nail polish, plaster on wood;
15 x 4½"

Nancy Davidson

Mix & Match, 1993
Fabric, wire, stretchers;
5 parts, 36 x 22 x 4" each
Courtesy Richard Anderson Fine
Arts, New York and Sue Spaid Fine
Art, Los Angeles
Overly Natural, 1993
Latex, fabric, wire;
3 parts, 60" diameter each
Courtesy Richard Anderson Fine
Arts, New York and Sue Spaid Fine
Art, Los Angeles
Souvenir, 1993
30 plastic bowling balls, 30 steel pad-
locks; 300" long
Courtesy Richard Anderson Fine
Arts, New York and Sue Spaid Fine
Art, Los Angeles

Kim Dingle

Gunball Machine, 1991
Mixed media; 7 x 38 x 12"
Collection Eileen and Peter Norton,
Santa Monica
Big Babies (inner tube legs), 1993
Oil on canvas; 72 x 60"
Courtesy of the artist and Kim Light
Gallery, Los Angeles
Wild Girls (striped dress), 1993
Oil on linen; 26 x 26"
Collection Al Gillio and Scott Durkin
Wild Girls (with glasses and oxfords),
1993
Oil on linen; 72 x 60"
Collection Eileen and Peter Norton,
Santa Monica

Jeanne Dunning

Untitled Hole, 1991-93
Cibachrome mounted to plexiglas,
frame; 25½ x 25½"
Courtesy Feature, New York
Untitled Hole, 1991-93
Cibachrome mounted to plexiglas,
frame; 25½ x 25½"
Courtesy Feature, New York
Untitled Hole, 1991-93
Cibachrome mounted to plexiglas,
frame; 25½ x 25½"
Courtesy Feature, New York
Flaw, 1993
Neoprene latex; 37 x 16½ x 16½"
Courtesy Feature, New York
Flaw, 1993
Neoprene latex; 37 x 16½ x 16½"
Courtesy Feature, New York
Flaw, 1993
Neoprene latex; 37 x 16½ x 16½"
Courtesy Feature, New York

Nancy Dwyer

Big Ego, 1990
Polyurethane nylon (yellow)
3 parts, 96 x 88 x 56" each

Courtesy of the artist and Josh Baer
Gallery, New York

Nicole Eisenman

Faux Bas, 1994
Ink charcoal, pencil;
144"x 180"
Courtesy Shoshana Wayne Gallery,
Santa Monica

Stephanie Ellis

Jackie Monroe Dress, 1992
Polished cotton; 96 x 36"
Pink Satin Panties, 1992
Satin; 72 x 108"

Sylvie Fleury

Private Lesson, 1992
Found videotape; 4 x 7⅜ x 1"
Courtesy Postmasters Gallery,
New York

Charles Gute

**Ludwig van Beethoven Needlepoint
Quotation #2: March 15, 1823, In a
Letter to Cherubini,** 1988
Dyed polyester rug yarn,
plastic canvas; 29½ x 15½"
Collection Marion Brenner and
Robert Harshorn Shimshak,
Berkeley, California
**Ludwig van Beethoven Needlepoint
Quotation #3: July 17, 1812, To a Very
Young Admirer (Ten Years Old),** 1988
Dyed polyester rug yarn, plastic
canvas; 18 x 30½"
Courtesy of the artist and Christopher
Grimes Gallery, Santa Monica
**Ludwig van Beethoven Needlepoint
Quotation #4: September 24, 1826, To
Breuning in the Schonbrunner Garden,**
1988
Dyed polyester rug yarn, plastic
canvas; 16 x 21"

Collection Nayland Blake,
San Francisco
**Ludwig van Beethoven Needlepoint
Quotation #5: August 11, 1810, To
Bettina von Arnim,** 1988
Dyed polyester rug yarn, plastic
canvas; 14 x 35"
Collection Dawn Fryling,
San Francisco
**Ludwig van Beethoven Needlepoint
Quotation #8: July 17, 1812, To an
Admirer Ten Years Old,** 1989
Dyed polyester rug yarn, plastic
canvas; 18 x 57"

Jacqueline Hayden

Figure Model Series, 1992
Gelatin silver print; 77 x 52"
Courtesy of the artist and Howard
Yezerski Gallery, Boston
Figure Model Series, 1991
Gelatin silver print; 74½ x 52"
Courtesy of the artist and Howard
Yezerski Gallery, Boston
Figure Model Series, 1991
Gelatin silver print; 85 x 52"
Courtesy of the artist and Howard
Yezerski Gallery, Boston

Marisa Hernandez

Ball Pouch, 1993
Velvet, satin, binder hooks, sinkers;
8 x 8 x 4"
Courtesy Terrain Gallery,
San Francisco
Swing, 1993
Velvet, satin, hardware; 15 x 60 x 6"
Courtesy Terrain Gallery,
San Francisco
Valance Strap and Crushed Grapes,
1993
Velvet, plastic fruit, hardware;
60 x 35 x 4"
Courtesy Terrain Gallery,
San Francisco

Margaret Honda

Dish, 1994
Mixed media installation with table settings and poison; 120 x 216 x 216"
Courtesy Shoshana Wayne Gallery, Santa Monica

Deborah Kass

Four Barbras, 1992
Acrylic on canvas; 20 x 24"
Collection Jeanne Meyers, Los Angeles
Single Silver Yentls, 1992-93
Acrylic on canvas;
3 parts: 72 x 36" each
Courtesy Jose Freire Fine Art, New York

Rachel Lachowicz

Untitled (Lipstick Urinals), 1992
Lipstick, wax, hydrocal;
3 parts, 15 x 9 x 6" each
Courtesy Shoshana Wayne Gallery, Santa Monica

Lauren Lesko

Lips, 1993
Fur collars;
4 parts, 12 x 6 x 1½" each
Collection Dean Sameshima, Los Angeles,
Coifed, 1993
Mixed media installation;
Couch 30 x 31 x 76", brocade-covered duvet 4 x 92 x 52"
Courtesy of the artist and Lipton Owens Company, New York

Jean Lowe

Private Collection, 1993
Mixed-media installation;
131 x 132 x 204"

Marlene McCarty

Campfire, 1992
Matchbooks and fur; 78" diameter
Courtesy of the artist and Metro Pictures, New York
Untitled, from the Immaculate Collection (I Fucked Madonna), 1992
Heat transfer on canvas; 72 x 48 x 6"
Courtesy of the artist and Metro Pictures, New York
Untitled (BOOB), 1993
Heat transfer on canvas; 84 x 84"
Collection Gloria and Robert Conn, Los Angeles

Jennie Nichols

Giant Rickrack, 1990
Human hair and thread;
30 x 48½ x 1"
Hair Balls, 1991
Human hair, knob, felt, styrofoam;
34 x 26 x 13"
Twin Toupee, 1993
Human hair, felt, frames, metal;
31 x 58 x 14½"
Collection Robert J. Shiffler, Greenville, Ohio

Gay Outlaw

Goosebump Chair, 1993
Wood, latex, upholstery materials;
38 x 38 x 37"
Webbed Plunger, 1993
Photogravure; 39¼ x 29⅞"
Skillet Pillar/Spinal Column, 1993
Polyurethane rubber, wood;
108 x 17 x 17"

Manuel Pardo

Artist's Self-Portrait: Mother's Dress #1, 2, and 3, 1993
Oil on birch plywood, hardware;
3 parts, 36 x 30 x 4" each

Theresa Pendlebury

Living Room, 1994
Mixed media installation;
120 x 192 x 168" overall; comprised of the following:
Black Cloud, 1991
Mohair; 10½ x 15 x 12"
Courtesy of the artist and Thomas Solomon's Garage, Los Angeles
Black Mail, 1991
Velvet envelopes, ribbon;
7 x 10 x 6½"
Collection Santa Barbara Museum of Art; Museum Purchase with funds provided by the Friends of Contemporary Art and the 20th Century Fund
Black Mood, 1991
Crochet yarn; 3¾ x 5½ x 5"
Private collection, courtesy Thomas Solomon's Garage, Los Angeles
Dark as Sin, 1991
Illuminated globe, lace; 16 x 11"
Collection Eileen and Peter Norton, Santa Monica
Dark Thoughts, 1991
Journals, flocking; 5½ x 9½ x 7"
Courtesy of the artist and Thomas Solomon's Garage, Los Angeles
Doily du Mal, 1991
Crochet cotton; 30 x 40"
Collection Eileen and Peter Norton, Santa Monica
My Black Heart, 1991
Foam, sequins, beads;
7½ x 4½ x 7¾"
Collection Lorrin and Deane Wong, Los Angeles
Secrets Absorbed, 1992
Velvet and paper covered desk blotter, pencil holder, pen, paper;
10 x 19 x 24"
Courtesy of the artist and Thomas Solomon's Garage, Los Angeles
Scream and Scream Again, 1991
Velvet, wood frames;
2 parts, 17 x 17" each

Collection Eileen and Peter Norton,
Santa Monica
Together Again, 1991
Ceramic, silicone;
2 teacups, 3½ x 2¾" each; teapot,
5½ x 8½ x 4¾"
Collection Betty Asher, Los Angeles
Halcyon Days, 1992
Black velvet photo album, black
photos; 10¾ x 9 x 1" (closed)
Courtesy of the artist and Thomas
Solomon's Garage, Los Angeles
Black Narcissus, 1992
Mirror, glass, enamel, acrylic, frame;
16½ x 23"
Collection Ami Arnault, Pasadena,
California
Urn, 1994
Crystal, ashes, wishbones, roses,
ribbons; 12½" high
Courtesy of the artist and Thomas
Solomon's Garage, Los Angeles
Curtains, 1994
Chiffon, dimensional paint, curtain
rod; 78 x 72"
Courtesy of the artist and Thomas
Soloman's Garage, Los Angeles

Rona Pondick

Double Bed, 1989
Mixed media; 9 x 73 x 162"
Courtesy of the artist and Jose Freire
Fine Art, New York
Milkman, 1989
Wax, plastic, canvas pillow, baby
bottles, shoes; 18½ x 34 x 22½"
Collection Ruth and Jacob Bloom,
Santa Monica
Loveseat, 1992
Wood, wax, plastic, lace, nipples;
17 x 25 x 12"
Courtesy Jose Freire Fine Art,
New York
Nipple Swing I, 1993
Shoes, lace, plastic, nipple, wire,
ribbon; 6¼ x 2¾ x 28½"

Courtesy Jose Freire Fine Art,
New York
Nipple Swing II, 1993
Shoes, lace, plastic, nipple, wire,
ribbon; 6¼ x 2¾ x 28½"
Courtesy Jose Freire Fine Art,
New York

Lucy Puls

**Manuballista Ignivoma Tres
(Three Rifles)**, 1993
Resin, toy guns, steel, pigments;
27 x 29 x 3"
Courtesy Stephen Wirtz Gallery,
San Francisco
Potestas Simplex (Plain Power), 1993
Steel, wigs; 40 x 10 x 10"
Courtesy Stephen Wirtz Gallery,
San Francisco
**Soleae Ninja Testudo (Ninja Turtle
Slippers)**, 1993
Resin, child's slippers, steel;
16 x 4 x 4"
Collection Stephen and Connie
Wirtz, Oakland, California
Summa Perfectionis Species (Brooke),
1993
Doll head, synthetic hair, steel,
thread; 88 x 16 x 7"
Courtesy Stephen Wirtz Gallery,
San Francisco
Tesserae Brooke (Brooke Blocks), 1993
Cardboard box, wood, plexiglas, syn-
thetic hair, plastic accessories,
polyester carpet; 11 x 60 x 60"
Courtesy Stephen Wirtz Gallery,
San Francisco

Trudie Reiss

**The History of Women in
Psychoanalysis, Part III**, 1993
Oil paint, polymer resin on canvas;
8 x 10"
Private collection, courtesy Kim Light
Gallery, Los Angeles

Domestic Violence, 1991
Oil paint, polymer resin on canvas;
8 x 10"
Collection Zoë and Joel Dictrow,
New York
Happy Family, 1992
Oil paint, polymer resin on canvas;
8 x 10"
Collection Dan Halsted, Burbank,
California
I Am a Hero II, 1992
Oil paint, polymer resin on canvas;
8 x 10"
Collection Colin Cowie and Stuart
Brownstein, Los Angeles
Unrequited Love, 1992
Oil paint, polymer resin on canvas;
10 x 8"
Private collection, courtesy Kim Light
Gallery, Los Angeles
The Inevitable Impossibility, 1993
Oil paint, polymer resin on canvas;
10 x 8"
Collection Geri and Arnie Obler,
Great Neck, New York

Erika Rothenberg

Men (West Coast), 1993
Mixed media installation;
80 x 94 x 60"
Courtesy of the artist and Rosamund
Felsen Gallery, Los Angeles

Beverly Semmes

Famous Twins, 1993
Cotton, crushed rayon velvet
2 parts, 140 x 48" each
Collection Zoë and Joel Dictrow,
New York

Lorna Simpson

Landscape/Body: Part I, 1992
Color polaroids, engraved plexiglas;
49½ x 20½"

Elena Sisto

Untitled, 1991
Watercolor, casein on paper; 10 x 13"
Collection Maria Porges,
Oakland, California

Untitled, 1991
Tempera on linen; 17 x 34"
Courtesy of the artist and Germans
Van Eck Gallery, New York

Untitled, 1992
Tempera on linen; 14 x 36" (diptych)
Courtesy of the artist and Germans
Van Eck Gallery, New York

The Look, 1992
Tempera on linen; 17 x 29"
Courtesy of the artist and Germans
Van Eck Gallery, New York

Pink and Black, 1992
Tempera on wood; 37 x 16½"
Courtesy of the artist and Germans
Van Eck Gallery, New York

Untitled, 1992
Watercolor, casein, fur on paper;
9½ x 12½"
Courtesy of the artist and Germans
Van Eck Gallery, New York

Jennifer Steinkamp

Untitled, 1994
Video projected animation, LCD
video projectors, 2 mirrors,
suspended cloth; 144 x 120 x 96"
Courtesy of the artist and Food
House, Santa Monica

Anne Walsh

Template, 1990
Embossed paper;
7 parts, 6 x 4½" each

Legend, 1992
Ink on paper, chewed foam rubber;
10½ x 35½ x 1½"
Collection Eileen and Peter Norton,
Santa Monica

Pass, 1992
20 pairs of the artist's shoes;
180 x 9 x 9"

she is me ELOISE, 1992-93
Pencil, ink on vellum, chewed and
clawed foam rubber;
6 parts, 11½ x 10 x 1" each

Megan Williams

Cherubs Pointing, 1990
Pastel on paper; 20 x 26"

Piece of Ass Sundae, 1992
Pastel on paper; 10 x 14"
Collection Clyde and Karen Beswick

Girl Looking, 1992
Pastel on paper;
15½ x 18½"
Courtesy of the artist and Christopher
Grimes Gallery, Santa Monica

He/She, 1992
Pastel, charcoal on paper; 15½ x 13"
Collection Karin Bravin, New York

Muscle Man, 1992
Pastel on paper; 13 x 9"
Courtesy Bravin Post Lee Gallery,
New York

S/B, 1992
Pastel on paper; 30 x 24"
Courtesy Bravin Post Lee Gallery,
New York

Boys Farting #2, 1993
Pastel on paper; 20 x 26"
Collection Patricia A. Bell

Rag Doll, 1993
Pastel on paper; 26 x 20"
Courtesy of the artist and
Christopher Grimes Gallery, Santa
Monica

Silenus, 1993
Charcoal, pastel on paper;
28 x 22"
Collection Clyde Beswick,
Los Angeles

Fountain, 1993
Pastel on paper; 26 x 20"

Courtesy of the artist, Christopher
Grimes Gallery, Santa Monica; and
Bravin Post Lee Gallery, New York

Sue Williams

Manly Footwear, 1992
Silicone rubber; 120 x 36" overall
Collection Tom Patchett, Los Angeles

Millie Wilson

Hood, 1993
Velvet, satin, plexiglas; 44 x 27"
Courtesy of the artist and Ruth
Bloom Gallery, Santa Monica

Bad Girls Video Checklist

Organized by Cheryl Dunye

All works are courtesy of the artist unless otherwise noted.

Program 1: She Laughed When She Saw It

total running time: 109 ½ min.

Tomboychik
Sandi DuBowski
1993, video, 15 min.

Street Walk
Kimberly Stoddard
1992, 16mm film, 2½ min.

Strut
Heidi DeRuiter
1992, 16mm film, b/w, 1 min.

I've Never Danced the Way Girls Were Supposed To
Dawn Suggs
1992, video, 8 min.
Courtesy of the artist and
Third World News Reel

Love, Boys and Food
Lee Williams/Angela Anderson
1993, video, 10 min.

Grapefruit
Cecilia Dougherty
1990, video excerpt, 20 min.
Courtesy Video Data Bank

Free Bird
Suzie Silver
1993, video, 11 min.
Courtesy Video Data Bank

War On Lesbians
Jane Cottis
1992, video excerpt, 15 min.
Courtesy Video Data Bank

Pet, Fluffy, Cheezy, Bunny . . .
Alix Pearlstein, 1993, video, 6 min.
Courtesy of the artist and Postmasters
Gallery, New York

God Gave Us Eyes
Elzabeth Beer/Agatha Kenar
1993, video, 12 min.

My Courbet or A Beaver's Tale
Mary Patten
1992, video, 9 min.

Program 2: Female Friends

total running time: 107 min.

The Scary Movie
Peggy Ahwesh
1991, Super 8mm film, 9 min.

The Fairies
Tom Rubnitz
1989, video, 7 min.
Courtesy Video Data Bank

Girl Power
Sadie Benning
1993, video, 15 min.
Courtesy Video Data Bank

My Penis
Lutz Bacher
1992, video, 3 min.

Glenda and Camille Do Downtown
Glenn Belverio
1993, video, 15 min.

Bicycle
Meryl Perlson
1992, video, 2 min.

Chronicles of a Lying Spirit
Cauleen Smith
1992, 16mm film, 6 min.
Courtesy of the artist and
Drift Distributions

I am a Famous French Director
Mira Gelley
1993, video, 16 min.

Brains on Toast
Liss Platt/Joyan Saunders
1992, video, 24 min.

Dangerous When Wet
Diane Bonder
1992, video, 5 min.

My American Friend
Cheng Sim Lim
1989, video, 5 min.
Courtesy Video Data Bank

Bad Girls Exhibitions Compendium

by Daniell Cornell

The Compendium is a representative rather than exhaustive listing of exhibitions that have been organized around feminist issues during the last three years. It is meant to suggest the wide range of feminist-related art projects, primarily in the U.S., in order to contextualize the works in *Bad Girls*. The focus is on American artists in order to keep the list representative of the exhibition. Due to the number of solo exhibitions organized around feminist concerns in recent years, it became necessary to limit the compendium to group shows, with the exception of a very few solo exhibitions that seemed especially suited to the concerns in *Bad Girls*. I have also tried to focus on smaller galleries and exhibition spaces not usually listed in catalogue compendiums in order to suggest the extent to which the concerns mobilized in the exhibition resonate throughout the country. Thanks especially to those smaller, independent organizations and spaces who helped compile this list.

1990

All but the Obvious
organized by Pam Gregg, L.A.C.E. (Los Angeles Contemporary Exhibitions), Los Angeles.

Biological Factors
Nexus Contemporary Art Center, Atlanta, Ga.

Celebrating the July 4, 1995 Demise of Patriarchy
organized by SisterSerpents, Edge of the Lookingglass, Chicago.

The Decade Show: Frameworks of Identity in the 1980s
organized by The Museum of Contemporary Hispanic Art, New York, The New Museum of Contemporary Art, New York, and The Studio Museum in Harlem, New York.

Domestic Disorders
Diverse Works, Houston, Tex.

Figuring Eros
Snug Harbor Cultural Center, Staten Island, New York.

Gigantic Women, Minature Works
Gallery 2, Chicago.

Projections in Public: A Storefront Window Exhibition
organized by Karen Atkinson, Spaces, Cleveland, Ohio.

Rattle Your Rage— Art By and For Oppressed Women
organized by SisterSerpents, Chicago, Filmmakers, Chicago, ABC No Rio, New York, and Kunstlerhaus, Hamburg, Germany.

Sacred Forces: Contemporary and Historical Images of the Goddess
organized by Andy Ostheimer, San Jose State University Gallery One, San Jose, Cal.

To Soar
presented in conjunction with a symposium, *Juxtapositions: The Art of Nancy Spero*, Smith College Museum of Art, Northampton, Mass.

A Woman's Life Isn't Worth Much
Franklin Furnace, New York.

1991

Challenging Myths: Five Contemporary Artists
organized by Heather Sealy Lineberry, Bakersfield Museum of Art, Bakersfield, Cal.

Chickens, Teapots, and More Than One Uterus
Vanderbult University Fine Arts Gallery, Nashville, Tenn.

Choice
A.I.R. Gallery, New York.

Dorothy Cross: Power House
Institute of Contemporary Art, Philadelphia, Penn.

Embodiment
organized by Angela Kelly, Randolph Street Gallery, Chicago.

Erotic Drawings
Artspace, San Francisco.

Helen Chadwick: De Light
Institute of Contemporary Art, Philadelphia, Penn.

Home for June
organized by Erik Oppenheim, Home for Contemporary Theater and Art, New York.

Margin of Safety
Musuem of Contemporary Art, Chicago.

New Generations: New York
organized by Elaine King, Carnegie Mellon Art Gallery, Pittsburgh, Penn.

No Laughing Matter
organized by Nina Felshin for Independent Curators, Inc., New York.

No More Heros: Unveiling Masculinity
organized by Barbara DeGenevieve, San Francisco Camerawork, San Francisco.

Outspoken Women: Heated Treatments in the '90s
Neuberger Museum, Purchase, N.Y., and Intermedia Arts, Minneapolis, Minn.

Ovarian Warriors vs. The Knights of Crissum
Sue Spaid Fine Art with Parker Zanic Gallery, Los Angeles.

Physical Relief
Bertha and Karl Leubsdorf Art Gallery, Hunter College, New York.

Piss on Passivity/Piss on Patriarchy
The Gallery, Chicago, and the EDGE, Denver, Col.

Plastic Fantastic Lover (Object A)
Blum Helman Warehouse, New York.

Pleasures and Terrors of Domestic Comfort
organized by Peter Galassi, Museum of Modern Art, New York.

Presswork: The Art of Women Printmakers
organized by Lang Communications, National Museum of Women in the Arts, Washington, D.C.

Scrap
Beaver College Art Gallery, Glenside, Penn.

Snakefest '91: Art Against Dickheads
Juried by SisterSerpents, Artemisia Gallery, Chicago.

Twisted Sisters
La Luz de Jesus, Los Angeles.

Who Cares About Femininism?: Art and Politics for the Nineties
A.I.R. Gallery, New York.

1992

Abortion a priori: Artists Support Row vs. Wade
ABC No Rio, New York.

The Abortion Project
organized by Kathe Burkhart and Chrysanne Stathacos with Anne R. Pasternak of RAW (Red Art Ways) Gallery, Hartford, Conn., and Hallwalls, Buffalo, N.Y.

Adios Columbus
organized by Miriam Hernandez and Regina Araujo Corritore of Vistas Latinas, Art in General, New York.

Ashley King, Lauren Szold, Sue Williams
303 Gallery, New York.

The Auto-Erotic Object
organized by Juli Carson, Hunter College Gallery, New York.

Ava Gerber/Anne Walsh/Sarah Whipple
organized by Irene Teatsos, N.A.M.E., Chicago.

Beverly Semmes
Sculpture Center, New York.

Counterweight: Alienation, Assimilation, Resistance
organized by Sondra Hale and Joan Hugo, Santa Barbara Contemporary Arts Forum, Santa Barbara, Cal.

Darkness Visible
The Drawing Center, New York.

Dirt and Domesticity: Constructions of the Feminine
Whitney Museum of American Art at Equitable Center, New York.

Disfunction in the Family Album
organized by David Humphrey, Diane Brown Gallery, New York.

Eva Hesse: A Retrospective
organized by Helen A. Cooper, Yale University Art Gallery, New Haven, Conn., and The Hirshhorn Museum and Scupture Center, Smithsonian Institution, Washington, D.C.

Fever
Exit Art, New York.

The Fortune Teller
Rochdale Art Gallery, Lancashire, U.K.

Funny Ha-Ha or Funny Peculiar?
fiction/nonfiction, New York.

Getting to kNOw you: Sexual Insurrection and Resistance
organized by Dean McNeil and Christophe Tannert, Kunstlerhaus Bethanien, Berlin.

The Lesbian Museum: 10,000 Years of Penis Envy
organized by Nicole Eisenman and Chris Martin, Franklin Furnace, New York.

Mistaken Identities
organized by Abigail Solomon-Godeau and Constance Lewallen, University of California Art Museum, Santa Barbara, Cal.

My Eyes Blur Sometimes, at Beauty
organized by Robert Lee, Asian American Arts Centre, New York.

The Politics of Difference: Artists Explore Issues of Identity
University Art Gallery, University of California, Riverside, Cal.

Radical Textiles
Southern Exposure, Project Artaud, San Francisco.

Re-Visions,
organized by Carole Tormollan and Angela Kelly, Randolph Street Gallery, Chicago.

Slouching Toward 2000: The Politics of Gender
organized by Lucy Lippard, Women and Their Work, Austin, Tex.

Speak
organized by Lynne Brown and Jin Lee, Randolph Street Gallery, Chicago.

Spew II
L.A.C.E. (Los Angeles Contemporary Exhibitions), Los Angeles.

Spellholle
organized by Kasper Konig and Robert Fleck, Akademie der Kunste und Wissenschaften, Frankfurt, Germany.

10: Artist as Catalyst
Alternative Museum, New York.

This is my body: this is my blood
organized by Susan E. Jahoda and May Stevens, Herter Art Gallery, University of Massachusetts, Amherst, Mass.

Voices of Freedom: Polish Women Artists and the Avant-Garde (1880-1990)
organized by Agnieszka Morawinska, the National Museum of Warsaw, and the National Museum of Women in the Arts, Washington, D.C.

Wall Drawings
The Drawing Center, New York.

Womenz Words
Coup de Grace Gallery, New York.

1993

The Art of Attack: Social Comment and its Effect
organized by the Wight Art Gallery, UCLA for The Armand Hammer Museum, Los Angeles.

Auto: On the Edge of Time
organized by Suzanne Lacy with the Niagara County Family Violence Coalition, Artpark, Lewiston, N.Y.

Backtalk
organized by Erica Daborn and Marilu Knode, Santa Barbara Contemporary Arts Forum, Santa Barbara, Cal.

Bad Girls
organized by Kate Bush, Emma Dexter, and Nicola White, Institute of Contemporary Arts, London.

Body Count
organized by Jan Avgikos, White Columns, New York.

Body Parts
Haines Gallery, San Francisco.

Carrie Mae Weems
organized by Susan Fisher Sterling and Andrea Kirsh, National Museum of Women in the Arts, Washington, D.C.

Coming to Power: 25 years of Sexually Explicit Art by Women
organized by Ellen Cantor, David Zwirner Gallery, New York and RAW (Real Art Ways) Gallery, Hartford, Conn.

Confessional
organized by Andrea Scott, Elizabeth Koury Gallery, New York.

Contexts and Identities
OK Hotel, Seattle, Wash.

Currents '93: Dress Codes
Insitute of Contemporary Art, Boston.

Die Arena Des Privaten
Kunstverein Munchen, Munich, Germany.

Disorderly Conduct
organized by Nina Felshin and Wendy Olsoff, P.P.O.W., New York.

Distinctive Dress
John Michael Kohler Arts Center, Sheboygan, Wisc.

The Feminine Mystique: Males Exploring Gender Boundaries
organized by Hellen Strong, Berta Walker Gallery, Provincetown, Mass.

Girlfriend in a Coma
Deseo Foundation, Mexico City, Mexico.

Home Noir
Organized by Linda Herritt, Boulder Art Center, Boulder, Colo.

In Search of Self
organized by Lisa Costantino and Valerie Hillings, Duke University Musuem of Art, Durham, NC.

In/Site 92
organized by the Arts Advisory Board of The Installation Gallery, Palomar College, San Marcos, Cal.

. . . Just to name a few
Galerie Barbara Weiss, Berlin.

Lutz Bacher: 'Jim and Sylvia'
MATRIX #155, University of California, Berkeley Art Museum, Berkeley, Cal.

Ladies Lunch: Exploring the Tradition
Louisville Visual Art Association, Ky.

Mechanical Brides: Women and Machines from Home to Office
organized by Ellen Lupton, Cooper-Hewitt Museum, New York.

Mirror, Mirror: Gender Roles and the Historical Significance of Beauty
organized by Terri Cohn, San Jose Institute of Contemporary Art, San Jose, Cal.

Mistaken Identities
organized by Abigail Solomon-Godeau and Constance Lewallen, University of California Art Museum, Santa Barbara, Cal.

1920: The Subtlety of Subversion, The Continuity of Intervention
Exit Art, New York.

The New World (Dis)Order
organized by Sidra Stich for the Northern California Council of the National Museum of Women's Art, and Yerba Buena Center for the Arts, San Francisco.

Playing House.
organized by Sharon Garbe and Holly Morse, Nathalie Karg Gallery, New York.

Privacy
organized by Gianni Romano, Documentario, Milan.

Private and Public Pleasures
organized by Lauren Lesko, Nomadic Site at The Newberry School of Beauty (storefront installation), Los Angeles.

Pro Femina:
Images of Women by Women
organized by Alison Devine Nordstrom and Patricia H. Snavely, Samuel P. Harn Museum of Art, University of Florida.

Re:Framing the Past, Recent Work from Texas Women Photographers
organized by Jean Caslin, The Houston Center for Photography, Houston, Tex.

Regarding Masculinity
Arthus Roger Gallery, New Orleans, La.

Sensual Disturbances: Judie Bamber, Jeanne Dunning, Patricia Bellen-Gillen
Tyler School of Art, Temple Univeristy, Philadelphia, Penn.

The Seventh Wave
organized by Stephen Foster, John Hansard Gallery, University of Southampton, U.K.

S/he Wore..., Shams, Mommy's Boy, Daddy's Girl, and A World of My Own
organized by Jon Winst for Southern Exposure, Project Artaud, San Francisco.

The Subject of Rape
Whitney Museum of American Art, New York.

Sugar 'n' Spice
organized by Noriko Gamblin and Carole Ann Klonarides, Long Beach Museum of Art. Long Beach, Cal.

Veiled Expectations
The Teahouse Gallery, New York, and Open Center, New York.

Women, Fire, and Iron
Wilensky Arts, Minneapolis, Minn.

Women Artists' Books, 1969-1979
Dia Center for the Arts Bookstore, New York, and Printed Matter bookstore, New York.

Women Artists of the Fifties
Anita Shapolsky Gallery, New York.

Women at War
LedisFlam, New York.

1994

After Perestroika: Kitchenmaids or Stateswomen
organized by Margarita Tupitsyn for Independent Curators, Inc., New York.

Cherry Bomb
organized by Mike Blockstein and Meg Mack for Southern Exposure, Project Artaud, San Francisco.

The Cross and the Crucifix
organized by Sepulveda Unitarian Universalist Society, Sepulveda, Cal.

DISEMBODIED: Recent Sculpture by Lesley Dill, Leslie Fry, and Elise Siegel
organized by Janie Cohen, Robert Hull Fleming Museum, University of Vermont, Burlington, Vt.

Empty Dress: Clothing as Surrogate in Recent Art
organized by Nina Felshin for Independent Curators, Inc., New York.

The First Generation: Women and Video, 1970-75
organized by JoAnn Hanley for Independent Curators, Inc., New York.

The Illustrated Woman: The Second Annual Conference on Feminist Activism and Art
San Francisco Camerawork, and The Forum at the Center for the Arts, Yerba Buena Gardens, San Francisco.

Keith Boadwee and Kent Howie
San Francisco Camerawork, San Francisco.

Menstruation
organized by Ann Boudreau, The Artist Alliance, Lafayette, LA.

No More Nice Girls
organized by Nicole Demeran, Spiral Arts, and ABC No Rio, New York.

Original Sinners: The Regiment of Women, An Erotic Art Show
organized by Kathryn Kirk, Cheryl Gross and Gail Goodman, Leslie Lohman Gay Art Foundation Gallery, New York.

Rebel Girls
 (Video program) organized by Jen Tait, Art Com, San Francisco.

Sense and Sensibility: Women and Minimalism in the Nineties
organized by Lynn Zelevansky, Museum of Modern Art, New York.

Who Is I?
organized by Sidra Stich, Yerba Buena Gardens Center for the Arts, San Francisco.

Women's Health
 A.I.R. Gallery, New York.

Bad Girls Bibliography

Compiled by Daniell Cornell

General

Bartkowski, Francis.
Feminist Utopias. Lincoln, Neb., and London: University of Nebraska Press, 1989.

Belenky, Mary Field, et al.
Women's Ways of Knowing: The Development of Self, Voice, and Mind. New York: Basic Books, 1986.

Brooks, Peter.
Body Work: Objects of Desire in Modern Narrative. Cambridge, Mass., and London: Harvard University Press, 1993.

Brown, Elaine.
A Taste of Power: A Black Woman's Story. New York: Pantheon Books, 1992.

Bulkin, Elly, Minnie Bruce Pratt and Barbara Smith.
Yours in Struggle: Three Feminist Perspectives on Anti-Semitism and Racism. Brooklyn, N.Y.: Long Haul Press, 1984.

Butler, Judith and Joan W. Scott, eds.
Feminists Theorize the Political. New York: Routledge, 1992.

Cambridge Women's Study Group.
Women In Society: Interdisciplinary Essays. London: Virago, 1981.

Cha, Theresa Hak Kyung, ed.
Dictée. New York: Tanam Press, 1982.
D' Erasmo, Stacey.
"Bad Girls Rule." *Village Voice* 34 (May 9, 1989): S15, S17.

Dargis, Manohla.
"Secret Vices: On Bad Girl Boots." *ArtForum* 30 (March 1992): 13-14.

Dent, Gina, ed.
Black Popular Culture: A Project by Michele Wallace. Seattle, Wash.: Bay Press, 1992.

Dolan, Jill.
The Feminist Spectator as Critic. Ann Arbor, Mich.: UMI Research Press, 1988.

Duggan, Lisa.
"Sex Panics." In *Democracy: A Project by Group Material.* Edited by Brian Wallis. Seattle, Wash.: Bay Press, 1990.

Echols, Alice.
Daring to Be Bad: Radical Feminism In America 1967-1975. Minneapolis: University of Minnesota Press, 1989.

English, Deirdre.
"The Fear that Feminism Will Free Men First." In *Democracy: A Project by Group Material.* Edited by Brian Wallis. Seattle, Wash.: Bay Press, 1990.

Faludi, Susan.
Backlash: The Undeclared War Against American Women. New York: Doubleday, 1991.

Gates, Henry Louis Jr., ed.
Reading Black, Reading Feminist. New York: Meridian Books, 1990.

Gates, Henry Louis Jr.
The Signifying Monkey: A Theory of African-American Literary Criticism. New York: Oxford University Press, 1988.

Giddings, Paula.
When and Where I Enter: The Impact of Black Women on Race and Sex in America. New York: Bantam Books, 1984.

Gilbert, Sandra M. and Susan Gubar.
"Sexchanges." *College English* 50 (November 1988): 768-785.

Greene Bayle and Coppelia Kahn, eds.
Making a Difference: Feminist Literary Criticism. London and New York: Methuen, 1985.

Heidenson, Frances M.
Women and Crime: The Life of the Female Offender. New York: New York University Press, 1985.

Heilbrun, Carolyn G.
Hamlet's Mother. New York: Columbia University Press, 1990.

Henderson, Mae Gwendolyn.
"Speaking In Tongues: Dialogics, Dialectics, and the Black Women Writer's Literary Tradition." In *Changing Our Own Words: Essays on Criticism, Theory and Writing by Black Women.* Edited by Cheryl A. Wall. New Brunswick, N.J. and London: Rutgers University Press, 1989.

hooks, bell.
"'When I Was a Young Soldier for the Revolution': Coming to Voice." In *Democracy: A Project by Group Material.* Edited by Brian Wallis. Seattle, Wash.: Bay Press, 1990.

hooks, bell.
Ain't I a Woman? Black Women and Feminism. Boston: South End Press, 1981.

hooks, bell.
Feminist Theory: From Margin to Center. Boston: South End Press, 1984.

Hull, Gloria T.
All the Women Are White, All the Blacks Are Men, But some of Us Are Brave: Black Women's Studies. Old Westbury, N.Y.: The Feminist Press, 1983.

Huyssen, Andreas.
"Mass Culture as Woman: Modernism's Other." In *Studies In Entertainment: Critical Approaches to Mass Culture.* Edited by Tania Modleski. Bloomington, Ind.: Indiana University Press, 1986.

Jacobs, Mary et. al., eds.
Body/Politics: Women and the Discourses of Science. New York and London: Routledge, 1990.

June, Andrea and V. Vale, eds.
Angry Women. San Francisco: Re/Search Publications, 1991.

Kramarae, Cheris and Paula A. Treichler.
Amazons, Bluestockings, and Crones: A Feminist Dictionary. London: Pandora Press, 1992.

Lauter, Estella.
Women as Mythmakers. Poetry and Visual Art by Twentieth-Century Women. Bloomington, Ind.: University of Indiana Press, 1984.

Malson, Micheline et al., eds.
Feminist Theory in Practice and Process. Chicago and London: University of Chicago Press, 1986.

Meese, Elizabeth A.
(Ex)tensions: Re-Figuring Feminist Criticism. Urbana, Ill.: University of Illinois Press, 1990.

Meese, Elizabeth A.
Crossing the Double-Cross: The Practice of Feminist Criticism. Chapel Hill, N.C.: University of North Carolina Press, 1986.

Minh-ha, Trinh T.
When the Moon Waxes Red: Representation, Gender and Cultural Politics. New York: Routledge, Chapman and Hall, 1991.

Minh-ha, Trinh T.
Woman, Native, Other: Writing Postcoloniality and Feminism. Bloomington, Ind.: Indiana University Press, 1989.

Mitchell, Juliet and Ann Oakley.
What Is Feminism: A Reexamination. Oxford, U.K.: Blackwell, 1986.

Mohanty, Russo et al., eds.
Third World Women and the Politics of Feminism. Bloomington and Indianapolis: Indiana University Press, 1991.

Morrison, Toni, ed.
Race-ing Justice, En-gendering Power: Essays on Anita Hill, Clarence Thomas, and the Construction of Social Reality. New York: Pantheon Books, 1992.

Nicholson, Linda, ed.
Feminism/Postmodernism. New York: Routledge, 1990.

O'Neale, Sondra.
"Inhibiting Midwives, Usurping Creators: The Struggling Emergence of Black Women In American Fiction" In *Feminist Studies/Critical Studies.* Edited by Teresa de Lauretis. Bloomington, Ind.: Indiana University Press, 1986.

Paglia, Camille.
Sex, Art, and American Culture: Essays. New York: Vintage Books, 1992.

Paglia, Camille.
Sexual Personae: Art and Decadence from Nefertiti to Emily Dickinson. New York: Vintage Books, 1990.

Palmer, Phyllis.
Domesticity and Dirt: Housewives and Domestic Servants In the United States, 1920-1945. Philadelphia: Temple University Press, 1989.

Parker, Dorothy.
The Portable Dorothy Parker. Introduction by Brendan Gill. New York: Penguin Books, 1944; reprinted 1976.

Parker, Rozsika.
The Subversive Stitch: Embroidery and the Making of the Feminine. London: The Women's Press, 1986.

Penley, Constance and Andrew Ross, eds.
Technoculture. Minneapolis: University of Minnesota Press, 1991.

Petchesky, Rosalind Pollack.
"Fetal Images: The Power of Visual Culture in the Politics of Reproduction." *Feminist Studies* 13 (Summer 1987): 263-92.

Showalter, Elaine, ed.
The New Feminist Criticism: Essays on Women, Literature and Theory.
New York: Pantheon Books, 1985.

Smith, Barbara, ed.
Home Girls: A Black Feminist Anthology. New York: Kitchen Table: Women of Color Press, 1983.

Solomon-Godeau, Abigail.
"Living with Contradictions: Critical Practices In the Age of Supply-Side Aesthetics." In *Universal Abandon?: The Politics of Postmodernism.* Edited by Andrew Ross. Minneapolis: University of Minnesota Press, 1988: 191-213.

Spivak, Gayatri Chakravorty.
In Other Worlds: Essays In Cultural Politics. New York: Methuen, 1987.

Spivak, Gayatri Chakravorty.
Outside In the Teaching Machine. New York: Routledge, 1993.

Women's Action Coalition.
WAC Stats: The Facts About Women. New York: The New Press, 1993.

Wall, Chery A.
Changing Our Own Words: Essays on Criticism, Theory and Writing by Black Women. New Brunswick, N.J. and London: Rutgers University Press, 1989.

Wallace, Michelle.
Invisibility Blues: From Pop to Theory. London: Verso, 1990.

Wolff, Janet.
Feminine Sentences: Essays on Women and Cutlure. Berkeley: University of California Press, 1990.

Art History

Allen, Paula Gunn.
The Sacred Hoop: Recovering the Feminine in American Indian Traditions. Boston: Beacon Press, 1986.

Ardener, Shirley, ed.
Women and Space: Ground Rules and Social Maps. New York: St. Martin's Press, 1981.

Ardener, Shirley, ed.
Persons and Powers of Women in Diverse Cultures: Essays in Commemoration of Audrey I Richards, Phyllis Kaberry, and Barbara E. Ward. New York: St. Martin's Press, 1992.

Armstrong, Carol.
Odd Man Out: Readings of the Work and Reputation of Edgar Degas. Chicago: University of Chicago Press, 1991.

Art Journal.
Special Issue: **"Feminist Art Criticism,"** 50 (Summer, 1991).

Betterton, Rosemary.
Looking On: Images of Femininity in the Visual Arts and Media. London: Pandora Press, 1987.

Brookner, Jackie.
"Feminism and Students of the '80s and '90s: The Lady and the Raging Bitch: or, How Feminism Got a Bad Name." *Art Journal* 50 (1991): 11-13.

Broude, Norma.
Impressionism: A Feminist Reading: The Gendering of Art, Science, and Nature In the Nineteenth Century. New York: Rizzoli, 1991.

Broude, Norma and Mary D. Garrard.
Feminism and Art History. New York: Harper and Row, 1982.

Bush, Kate et al., eds.
Bad Girls (exhibition catalogue). Organized by Kate Bush, Emma Dexter and Nicola White with essays by Laura Cottingham and Cherry Smyth. London: ICA, 1993.

Chadwick, Whitney.
Women, Art and Society. London: Thames and Hudson, 1990.

Chicago, Judy.
The Birth Project. Garden City, N.Y.: Doubleday, 1985.

Chicago, Judy and Susan Hill.
Embroidering Our Heritage: The Dinner Party Needlework. Garden City, N.Y.: Anchor, 1980.

Curiger, Bice.
Meret. Oppenheim: Defiance In the Face of Freedom. New York: PAR-KETT Pubs. and Cambridge, Mass.: MIT Press, 1989.

Ferguson, Russell et al., eds.
Discourses: Conversations In Postmodern Art and Culture. New York: The New Museum of Contemporary Art and Cambridge, Mass.: MIT Press, 1990.

Flomenhaft, Eleanor.
"Interviewing Faith Ringgold: A Contemporary Heroine." In *Faith Ringgold: A 25 Year Survey.* Edited by Eleanor Flomenhaft. New York: Simon and Schuster, 1979.

Foster, Hal, ed.
The Anti-Aesthetic: Essays on Post Modern Culture. Port Townsend, Wash.: Bay Press, 1983.

Foster, Hal, ed.
Recordings: Art, Spectacle, Cultural Politics. Port Townsend, Wash.: Bay Press, 1985.

Foster, Stephen, ed.
The Seventh Wave (exhibition catalogue). Southhampton, U.K.: John Hansard Gallery and London: Pale Green Press, 1993.

Garrard, Mary D. Artemisia
Gentileschi: The Image of the Female Hero In Italian Baroque Art.
Princeton, N.J.: Princeton University Press, 1989.

Gouma-Peterson, Thalia.
"Modern Dilemma Tales: Faith Ringgold's Story Quilts."
In *Faith Ringgold: A 25 Year Survey* (exhibition catalogue). Compiled by Eleanor Flomenhaft. New York: Simon and Schuster, 1979.

Gouma-Peterson, Thalia and Patricia Mathews.
"The Feminist Critique of Art History."
Art Bulletin 43 (September 1987): 326-57.

Haskell, Barbara and John G. Hanhardt.
Yoko Ono: Arias and Objects.
Salt Lake City, Utah: Peregrine Books, and Gibbs Smith Pub., 1991.

Higonnet, Anne.
Berthe Morisot's Images of Women.
Cambridge, Mass. and London: Harvard University Press, 1992.

hooks, bell.
Black Looks: Race and Representation.
Boston: South End Press, 1992.

Isaak, Jo Anna.
The Ruin of Representation in Modernist Art and Texts.
Ann Arbor, Mich.: UMI Research Press, 1986.

Kasson, Joy S.
Marble Queens and Captives: Women in Nineteenth-Century American Scupture. New Haven and London: Yale University Press, 1990.

Kristeva, Julia.
Desire In Language: A Semiotic Approach to Literature and Art.
Edited by Leon S. Roudiez. Translated by Thomas Gora et al. Oxford, U.K.: Basil Blackwell, 1981

Lippard, Lucy.
From the Center: Feminist Essays on Women's Art. New York: Dutton, 1976.

Lippard, Lucy.
"In the Flesh: Looking Back and Talking Back." *Women's Art Magazine* 54 (September/October 1993): 4-9; and in *Backtalk* (exhibition catalogue). Santa Barbara, Cal.: Santa Barbara Contemporary Art Forum, 1993.

Lippard, Lucy.
Mixed Blessings: New Art in a Multicultural America.
New York: Pantheon, 1990.

Lippard, Lucy.
Partial Recall: Photographs of Native North Americans. New York: The New Press, 1992.

Lippard, Lucy
"Sweeping Exchanges: The Contribution of Feminism to the Art of the Seventies." *Art Journal* 41 (1980).

Lipton, Eunice.
Alias Olympia: A Woman's Search for Manet's Notorious Model and Her Own Desire. New York: Charles Scribner's Sons, 1992.

McKenna, Kristine.
"Yoko Reconsidered." *Los Angeles Times, Calendar* (April 11, 1993).

Melosh, Barbara.
Engendering Culture: Manhood and Womanhood in New Deal Public Art and Theater. Washington, D.C.: Smithsonian Institution Press, 1991.

Munro, Eleanor.
Originals: American Women Artists.
New York: Simon and Schuster, 1979.

New Observations.
Special Issue edited by Adrian Piper: **"Color,"** 97 (September/October, 1993).

Nochlin, Linda.
Women, Art, and Power and Other Essays. New York: Harper and Row, 1988.

Nochlin, Linda.
The Politics of Vision: Essays on Nineteenth-Century Art and Society.
New York: Harper and Row, 1989.

Ono, Yoko.
Grapefruit. New York: Simon and Schuster, 1970.

Parker, Rozsika and Griselda Pollock.
Framing Feminism: Art and the Women's Movement, 1970-85.
London: Pandora, 1987.

Parker, Rozsika and Griselda Pollock.
Old Mistresses: Women, Art and Ideology. New York: Pantheon, 1981; reprinted London: Pandora, 1987.

Phillips, Lisa.
"Cindy Sherman's Cindy Shermans." In *Cindy Sherman* (exhibition catalogue). New York: Whitney Museum of American Art, 1987.

Pointon, Marcia.
Naked Authority: The Body In Western Painting 1830-1908. Cambridge, U.K.: Cambridge University Press, 1990.

Pollock, Griselda.
"Women, Art and Ideology: Questions for Feminist Art Historians."
Woman's Art Journal 4 (Spring/Summer 1983).

Pollock, Griselda.
"The History and Position of the Contemporary Woman Artist."
Aspects 28 (1984).

Pollock, Griselda.
Vision and Difference: Femininity, Feminism and the Histories of Art.
London: Routledge, 1988.

Pollock, Griselda.
"Vision, Voice and Power: Feminist Art History and Marxism" *Block* 6 (1982): 6-9.

Porges, Maria.
"Openings: Rachel Lachowicz."
Artforum 31 (January 1993): 80.

Raven, Arlene et al., eds.
Feminist Art Criticism: An Anthology.
Minneapolis, Minn.: UMI Press, 1988; reprinted New York: Harper Collins, 1991.

Robins, Corinne.
"Why We Need 'Bad Girls' Rather Than 'Good' Ones!" In *M/E/A/N/I/N/G* 8 (November 1990): 43-48.

Robinson, Hilary, ed.
Visibly Female: Feminism and Art, An Anthology. New York: Universe Books, 1988.

Rosen, Randy and Catherine C. Brawer, eds.
Making Their Mark: Women Artists Move into the Mainstream, 1970-85 (exhibition catalogue). Organized by R. Rosen and C. C. Brawer. New York: Abbeville Press, 1989.

Rubinstein, Charlotte Streifer.
American Women Artists: From early Indian Times to the Present.
Boston: G. K. Hall and New York: Avon, 1982.

Slatkin, Wendy.
Women Artists In History: From Antiquity to the 20th Century.
Englewood Cliffs, N.J.: Prentice-Hall, 1985.

Smith, Roberta.
"The New Appropriationists: Engaging the Enemy." *New York Times* (August 16, 1992).

Smith, Roberta.
"Quilted Narratives."
New York Times (February 14, 1992).

Spector, Nancy.
"Neither Bachelors Nor Brides: The Hybrid Machines of Rebecca Horn." In *Rebecca Horn* (exhibition catalogue). New York: The Solomon R. Guggenheim Foundation, 1993.

Squires, Carol, ed.
The Critical Image: Essays on Contemporary Photography.
Seattle, Wash.: Bay Press, 1990.

Stewart, Susan.
On Longing: Narratives of the Miniature, the Gigantic, the Souvenir, the Collection. Durham, N.C.: Duke University Press, 1993.

Suleiman, Susan Rubin, ed.
The Female Body In Western Culture: Contemporary Perspectives.
Cambridge, Mass.: Harvard University Press, 1986.

Tickner, Lisa.
The Spectacle of Woman: Imagery of the Suffrage Campaign, 1907-14.
Chicago: University of Chicago Press, 1988.

Tucker, Marcia.
"An Iconography of Recent Figurative Painting: Sex, Death, Violence and the Apocalypse." *ArtForum* (Summer 1982).

Tucker, Marcia.
"Nancy Dwyer Makes Trubble."
ArtForum (November 1989).

Tucker, Marcia.
"Picture This: An Introduction to INTERIM." In *Mary Kelly, INTERIM* (exhibition catalogue). With Norman Bryson, Griselda Pollock, and Hal Foster. New York: The New Museum of Contemporary Art, 1990.

Wallis, Brian, ed.
Art After Modernism: Rethinking Representation. New York: The New Museum of Contemporary Art and Boston: Godine, 1984.

Wallis, Brian, ed.
Blasted Allegories: An Anthology of Writings by Contemporary Artists.
New York: The New Museum of Contemporary Art and Cambridge, Mass.: MIT Press, 1987.

Women's Art Magazine.
Special Issue: **"From Good Girls to Bad Girls: 20 Years of Feminist Art,"** 54 (September/October, 1993).

Wye, Deborah.
Louise Bourgeois (exhibition catalogue). New York: Museum of Modern Art, 1983.

Transgression and Subversion

Bakhtin, Mikhail.
Rabelais and His World.
Translated by Helene Iswolsky. Cambridge, Mass.: MIT University Press, 1968.

Bakhtin, Mikhail.
The Dialogic Imagination: Four Essays.
Edited by Michael Holquist. Translated by Caryl Emerson and Michael Holquist. Austin, Tex.: University of Texas Press, 1981.

Bataille, Georges.
The Tears of Eros. Translated by Peter Connor. Paris, 1961; reprinted San Francisco: City Lights, 1989.

Citron, Alan.
"Bumper Crop of Prostitute Films Due." *Los Angeles Times* (November 3, 1993).

Copjec, Joan.
"Flaviat et. Dissitati Sunt." *October* 18 (Fall 1981).

Ferguson, Russell, et al., eds.
Out There: Marginalization and Contemporary Cultures. New York: The New Museum of Contemporary Art and Cambridge, Mass.: MIT Press, 1990.

Fiedler, Leslie.
Freaks. New York: Touchstone Books, 1978.

Garber, Marjorie.
Vested Interests: Cross-Dressing and Cultural Anxiety. New York: Routledge, Chapman and Hall, 1992.

Gilman, Susan.
Difference and Pathology: Stereotypes of Sexuality, Race and Madness. Ithaca, N.Y.: Cornell University Press, 1985.

Gunderloy, Mike and Cari Goldberg Janice.
The World of Zines.
New York: Penguin, 1992.

Haraway, Donna.
"A Manifesto for Cyborgs."
In *Feminism/Postmodernism.*
Edited by Linda Nicholson. New York: Routledge, 1990.

Hatlen, Burton.
"Michel Foucault and the Discourse[s] of English." *College English* 50 (November 1988): 786-801.

Herron, Jerry.
On Feeling Blue: Sex, Reagonomics, Violence and Taboo. Bowling Green, Ohio: Bowling Green University Popular Press, 1984.

Hutcheon, Linda.
A Theory of Parody: The Teachings of Twentieth-Century Art Forms.
New York and London: Methuen, 1985.

Isaak, Jo Anna.
"Nancy Spero: A Work In Comic Courage." In *Nancy Spero, Works Since 1950.* Syracuse, N.Y.: Everson Museum of Art, 1987.

Keesey, Pam.
Daughters of Darkness: Lesbian Vampire Stories. Pittsburgh, Penn.: Cleis Press, 1993.

Lurie, Alison.
Don't Tell the Grown-ups: Subversive Children's Literature.
Boston: Little, Brown, 1990.

Maharaj, Sarat.
"Pop Art's Pharmacies: Kitsch, Consumerist Objects and Signs, The 'Unmentionable'." *Art History* 15 (September 1992): 334-350.

Marcus, Greil.
Lipstick Traces: A Secret History of the Twentieth Century. Cambridge, Mass.: Harvard University Press, 1989.

Richter, David H., ed.
The Critical Tradition.
New York: St. Martin's Press, 1989.

Russo, Mary.
"Female Grotesques: Carnival and Theory." In *Feminist Studies/Critical Studies.* Edited by Teresa de Lauretis. Bloomington, Ind.: Indiana University Press, 1986.

Scholder, Amy and Ira Silverberg, eds. **High Risk: An Anthology of Forbidden Writings.** New York: Plume, 1991.

Shift.
Special Issue by San Francisco Art Space: **"Fifteen,"** 7 (1993).

Stallybrass, Peter and Allon White. **The Politics and Poetics of Transgression.** Ithaca, N.Y.: Cornell University Press, 1986.

Stam, Robert. **Subversive Pleasures: Bakhtin, Cultural Criticism, and Film.** Baltimore, Md.: The Johns Hopkins University Press, 1989.

Suleiman, Susan Rubin. **Subversive Intent: Gender, Politics and the Avant-Garde.** Cambridge, Mass.: Harvard University Press, 1990.

Swezey, Stuart and Brian King, eds. **Amok: Sourcebook of the Extremes of Information In Print.** Los Angeles: Fourth Dispatch, 1990.

Tallman, Susan. **"Guerrilla Girls."** *Arts Magazine* 65 (April 1991): 21-22.

Tamblyn, Christine. **"No More Nice Girls: Recent Transgressive Feminist Art."** *Art Journal* 50 (1991): 53-57.

Tucker, Marcia. **"Bad" Painting** (exhibition catalogue). Organized by Marcia Tucker. New York: The New Museum of Contemporary Art, 1978.

Tucker, Marcia. **Choices: Making an Art of Everyday Life** (exhibition catalogue). Organized by Marcia Tucker. New York: The New Museum of Contemporary Art, 1986.

Tucker, Marcia. **Not Just For Laughs: The Art of Subversion** (exhibition catalogue). Organized by Marcia Tucker. New York: The New Museum of Contemporary Art, 1982.

Tucker, Michael. **Dreaming With Open Eyes: The Shamanic Spirit In Twentieth-Century Art and Culture.** San Francisco: Aquarian/Harper, 1992.

Humor

Barreca, Regina, ed. **Last Laugh: Perspectives on Women and Comedy.** New York: Gordon and Breach, 1988.

Barreca, Regina. **They Used to Call Me Snow White— But I Drifted: Women's Strategic Use of Humor.** New York: Viking, 1991.

Bloomingdale, Teresa. **Sense and Momsense.** Garden City, N.Y.: Doubleday, 1986.

Cole, Caroline M. **"Oh Wise Women of the Stalls."** *Discourse and Society* 91 (October): 401-11.

DiMassa, Diane. **Hothead Paisan: Homicidal Lesbian Terrorist.** Pittsburgh, Penn.: Cleis Press, 1993.

Heimel, Cynthia. **Get Your Tongue Out of My Mouth, I'm Kissing you Good-bye.** New York: Simon and Schuster, 1992.

Kaufman, Gloria. **In Stitches: A Patchwork of Feminist Humor and Satire.** Bloomington, In.: Indiana University Press, 1991.

Maney, Mabel. **The Case of the Not-So-Nice Nurse.** Pittsburgh, Penn.: Cleis Press, 1993.

Natalie, Andrea. **Rubyfruit Mountain: A Stonewall Riots Collection.** Pittsburgh, Penn.: Cleis Press, 1993.

Schultz, Ellen E. **"Among the Bogobo"** *Savvy Woman* 11 (Dec 1990): 90, 89.
Sochen, June, ed. **Women's Comic Visions.** Detroit, Mich.: Wayne State University Press, 1991.

Walker, Nancy. **A Very Serious Thing: Women's Humor and American Culture.** Minneapolis: University of Minnesota Press, 1988.

Warren, Rosalind, ed. **Women's Glib.** Freedom, Cal.: The Crossing Press, 1990.

Media and Performance

Allen, Robert C.
Horrible Prettiness: Burlesque and American Culture. Chapel Hill, N.C.: University of North Carolina Press, 1991.

Altman, Rick.
"A Semantic/Syntactic Approach to Film Genre." In *Film Genre Reader.* Edited by Barry Keith Grant. Austin, Tex.: University of Texas Press, 1986: 26-40.

Andrew, Stephen.
"Are you now or have you ever been . . . a man?" *London Observer* (14 July 1991): 15

Bad Object Choices, ed.
"Film and the Visible." In *How Do I Look? Queer Film and Video.* Seattle, Wash.: Bay Press, 1991.

Carter, Erica.
ICA Documents: Black Film/British Cinema. London: Institute of Comtemporary Arts, 1988.

Case, Sue-Ellen, ed.
Performing Feminisms: Feminist Critical Theory and Theatre. Baltimore, Md.: The Johns Hopkins University Press, 1990.

Cha, Teresa Hak Kyung, ed.
Apparatus, Cinematographic Apparatus: Selected Writings. New York: Tanam Press, 1981.

Cham, Mbye B. and Claire Andrade-Watkins, eds.
Black Frames: Critical Perspectives on Black Independent Cinema. Boston: Celebration for Black Cinema, Inc., and Cambridge, Mass.: MIT Press, 1988.

Champagne, Leonara, ed.
Out From Under: Texts by Women Performance Artists. New York: TCG (Theater Communications Group), 1990.

Davy, Kate.
"Constructing the Spectator: Reception, Context, and Address In Lesbian Performance." *Performing Arts Journal* 10 (1986).

de Lauretis, Teresa.
Alice Doesn't: Feminism, Semiotics, Cinema. Bloomington, Ind.: Indiana University Press, 1984.

Dyer, Richard.
Heavenly Bodies: Film Stars and Society. London: Macmillan, 1986.

Frank, Lisa and Paul Smith, eds.
Madonnarama: Essays on Sex and Popular Culture. Pittsburgh, Penn. and San Francisco: Cleis Press, 1993.

Greenberg, Harvey R.
"'Thelma and Louise's' Exuberant Polysemy." *Film Quarterly* 45 (Winter 1991-1992): 20-21.

Hall, Doug and Sally Jo Fifer.
Illuminating Video: An Essential Guide to Video Art. San Francisco: Bay Area Video Coalition and Aperture, 1990.

Jump Cut, Special sections:
"Lesbians and Film," 24; 25 (1981).

Kinder, Marsha.
"'Thelma and Louise' and 'Messidor' as Feminist Road Movies." *Film Quarterly* 45 (Winter 1991-1992): 30-31.

Kuhn, A.
Women's Pictures: Feminism and the Cinema. London: Routledge and Kegan Paul, 1982.

Lewis, Lisa A.
Gender Politics and MTV: Voicing the Difference. Philadelphia: Temple University Press, 1990.

Lott, Eric.
Love and Theft: Blackface Minstrelsy and The American Working Class. Oxford, U.K.: Oxford University Press, 1993.

Mast, Gerald, et al.
Film Theory and Criticism: Introductory Readings. 4th Edition. New York: Oxford University Press, 1992.

McCabe, Colin, ed.
High Theory/Low Culture: Analyzing Popular Television and Film. New York: St. Martin's Press, 1986.

Modleski, Tania, ed.
Studies In Entertainment: Critical Approaches to Mass Culture. Bloomington, Ind.: Indiana University Press, 1986.

Noriega, Chon A., ed.
Chicanos and Film. Minneapolis: University of Minnesota Press, 1992.

Penley, Constance.
Feminism and Film Theory. New York: Routledge, 1988.

Pribram, E. Deidre.
Female Spectators: Looking At Film and Television. New York: Verso, 1989.

Studlar, Gaylyn.
In the Realm of Pleasure: Von Sternberg, Dietrich, and the Masochistic Aesthetic. Chicago: University of Illinois Press, 1988.

Williams, Linda.
Re-Vision: Essays In Feminist Film Criticism. Frederick, Md.: University Publications of America, 1984.

Williams, Linda.
"What Makes a Woman Wander." *Film Quarterly* 45 (Winter 1991-1992): 27-28.

Sexuality

Abelove, Henry, et al., eds.
The Lesbian and Gay Studies Reader. New York: Routledge, 1993.

Act Up/NY Women and AIDS Book Group.
Women, AIDS and Activism. New York: The Act Up/NY Women and AIDS Book Group, 1990.

Art + Text.
Special Issue edited by Kay Rosen and Joyce Hinterding: "Terrible Beauty, Wild Women," 46 (September 1993).

Barale, Michele Aina.
"Below the Belt: (Un)Covering The Well of Loneliness."
In *Inside/Out: Lesbian Theories, Gay Theories.* Edited by Diana Fuss. New York: Routledge, 1991: 235-257.

Benjamin, Jessica.
The Bonds of Love. New York: Pantheon, 1988.

Boone, Joseph A. and Michael Cadden, eds.
Engendering Men: The Question of Male Feminist Criticism. New York: Routledge, 1990.

Burgen, Victor et al., eds.
Formations of Fantasy. London and New York: Methuen, 1986.

Burroughs, Catherine B. and Jeffrey David Ehrenreich, eds.
Reading the Social Body. Iowa City: University of Iowa Press, 1993.

Butler, Judith.
Gender Trouble: Feminism and the Subversion of Identity. New York: Routledge, 1990.

Butler, Judith.
"The Force of Fantasy: Feminism, Mapplethorpe, and Discursive Excess." *differences* 2 (Summer 1990): 105-125.

Chua, Lawrence.
"On Queer Zines." *ArtForum* (October 1992): 9.

Clarke, David.
"The Gaze and the Glance: Competing Understandings of Visuality in the Theory and Practice of Late Modernist Art." *Art History* 15 (March 1992): 80-98.

Clayson, Hollis.
Painted Love: Prostitution In French Art of the Impressionist Era. New Haven and London: Yale University Press, 1991.

Colomina, Beatriz.
Sexuality and Space. Princeton, N.J.: Princeton Architectural Press, 1992.

Coward, Rosalind.
Female Desires. New York: Grove Press, 1985.

Cowie, E.
"Woman as Sign." *m/f* 1 (1978).

Crimp, Douglas.
"How to Have Promiscuity in an Epidemic." In *AIDS: Cultural Analysis, Cultural Activism.* Edited by Douglas Crimp. Cambridge, Mass.: MIT Press, 1988.

de Lauretis, Teresa.
Technologies of Gender: Essays on Theory, Film, and Fiction. Bloomington, Ind.: Indiana University Press, 1987.

differences: A Journal of Feminist Cultural Studies.
Special Issue edited by Teresa de Lauretis: "Queer Theory: Lesbian and Gay Sexualities," 3 (Summer 1991).

Doane, Mary Ann.
"Film and the Masquerade: Theorizing the Female Spectator." *Screen* 23 (1982): 74-87.

Echols, Alice.
"The New Feminism of Yin and Yang" In *Powers of Desire: The Politics of Sexuality.* Edited by Ann Snitow, Christine Stansell and Sharon Thompson. New York: Monthy Review Press, 1983.

Fernades, Joyce.
"Sex into Sexuality: A Feminist Agenda for the '90s." In *Art Journal* 50 (1991).

Fleming, L.
"Levi-Strauss, Feminism and the Politics of Representation." *Block* 9 (1983).

Frontiers: A Journal of Women's Studies. Special Issue: **"Lesbianism,"** 4 (Fall 1979).

Frueh, Joanna.
"Re-vamping the Vamp." *Arts Magazine* 42 (October 1982): 98-103.

Furman, Nelly.
"The Politics of Language: Beyond the Gender Principle?" In *Making a Difference: Feminist Literary Criticism.* Edited by Gayle Greene and Coppelia Kahn. London and New York: Methuen, 1985.

Fuss, Diana, ed.
Inside/Out: Lesbian Theories, Gay Theories. New York: Routledge, 1991.

Gamman, Lorraine and Margaret. Marshment, eds.
The Female Gaze: Women as Viewers of Popular Culture. Seattle, Wash.: The Real Comet Press, 1989.

Geever, Martha and Nathalie Magnan.
"The Same Difference: On Lesbian Representations." *Exposure* 24 (1986): 27-35.

GLQ: A Journal of Lesbian and Gay Studies.
Introductory Issue: essay by Eve Kosofsky Sedgwick, 1 (Fall 1993).

Hanson, Karen.
"Dressing Down Dressing Up—The Philosophic Fear of Fashion." *Hypatia* 5 (Summer 1990): 107-21.

Heresies.
Special Issue:
"The Sex Issue," 12 (1981).

hooks, bell.
"Men: Comrades In Struggle." In *Men's Lives.* Edited by Michael S. Kimmel. New York: Macmillan, 1987: 561-71.

Isaak, Jo Anna.
"Women—The Ruin of Representation." *Afterimage* 12 (1985).

Jameson, Frederic.
"Pleasure: A Political Issue." In *Formations of Pleasure.* Edited by Victor Burgin. London: Methuen, 1983: 1-14.

Jardine, Alice and Paul Smith, eds.
Men In Feminism. New York: Methuen, 1987.

Kelly, Mary.
"Desiring Images/Imaging Desire." *Wedge* 6 (1984).

Kelly, Mary.
"On Sexual Politics and Art." In *Framing Feminist Art and The Women's Movement, 1970-85.* Edited by R. Parker and G. Pollock. London: Pandora, 1987.

Kent, Sarah. and Jacqueline Morreau, eds.
Women's Images of Men.
New York: Writers and Readers Pub., 1985; reprinted London: Pandora, 1990.

Koestenbaum, Wayne.
The Queen's Throat: Opera, Homosexuality and the Mystery of Desire. New York: Poseidon Press, 1993.

Kotz, Liz.
"The Body You Want: Liz Kotz Interviews Judith Butler." *Artforum* (November 1992): 82-89.

Kroker, Arther and Marilouise, eds.
Body Invaders: Panic Sex in America. New York: St. Martin's Press, 1987.

Landry, Donna.
"Treating Him Like an Object: William Beatty Warner's 'Di(va)lution'." In *Feminism and Institutions.* Edited by Linda Kauffman. London: Basil Blackwell, 1989.

Linker, Kate.
Difference: On Representation and Sexuality. New York: The New Musuem of Contemporary Art, 1985.

Linker, Kate.
"Representation and Sexuality." In *Art After Modernism: Rethinking Representation.* Edited by Brian Wallis. New York: The New Museum of Contempoary Art, 1984.

Mathews, Patricia.
"What is Female Imagery?" *Women Artists News,* 10 (November 1984): 5-7.

Mayne, Judith.
"Lesbian Looks: Dorothy Arzner and Female Authorship." In *How Do I Look? Queer Film and Video.* Edited by Bad Object Choices. Seattle, Wash.: Bay Press, 1991: 103-145.

Modleski, Tania.
Feminism Without Men: Culture and Criticism in a "Postfeminist" Age. New York: Routledge, 1991.

Mulvey, Laura.
Visual and Other Pleasures. Bloomington, Ind.: Indiana University Press, 1989.

The New Museum of Contemporary Art. *Extended Sensibilities: The Impact of Homosexual Sensibilities on Contemporary Culture* (exhibition catalogue). Organized by Daniel J. Cameron. New York: The New Museum of Contemporary Art, 1982.

Owens, Craig. *Beyond Recognition: Representation, Power, and Culture.* Edited by Scott Bryson et al. Berkeley: University of California Press, 1992.

Owens, Craig. "The Discourse of Others: Feminism and Postmodernism." In *The Anti-Aesthetic.* Edited by Hal Foster. Port Townsend, Wash.: Bay Press, 1983: 57-82.

Owens, Craig. "The Medusa Effect or, The Specular Ruse." *Art In America* (January 1984): 97-106.

Rafkin, Louise, ed. *Different Mothers: Sons and Daughters of Lesbians Talk about Their Lives.* Pittsburgh, Penn.: Cleis Press, 1987.

Rich, Adrienne. *Women and Honor: Some Notes on Lying.* Pittsburgh, Penn.: Motheroot Pubs, 1977; reprinted by Cleis Press, 1992.

Saalfield, Catherine and Ray Navarro. "Shocking Pink Praxis: Race and Gender on the ACT UP Frontlines." In *Inside/Out: Lesbian Theories, Gay Theories.* Edited by Diana Fuss. New York: Routledge, 1991: 341-69.

Schneeman, Carolee. *More Than Meat Joy.* New Paltz, N.Y.: Documentext, 1979.

Schor, Mira. "Patrilineage." *Art Journal* 50 (1991): 58-64.

Snitow, Ann, et al., eds. *Powers of Desire: The Politics of Sexuality.* New York: Monthly Review Press, 1983.

Solomon-Godeau, Abigail. "Male Trouble: A Crisis In Representation." *Art History* 16 (June 1993): 286-312.

Strayer, Chris. "The She-man: Postmodern bi-sexed performance in film and video." *Screen* 31 (Autumn 1990): 262-81.

Tucker, Marcia. *The Other Man: Alternative Representations of Masculinity.* (exhibition brochure). Organized by Marcia Tucker. New York: The New Museum of Contemporary Art, 1987

Williamson, Judith. "A Piece of the Action: Images of 'Woman' In the Photography of Cindy Sherman." *Consuming Passions.* New York: Marion Boyars, 1986: 91-112.

Pornography and Censorship

Art Journal. Special Issues: "Censorship," 50 (Fall, 1991; Winter, 1992).

Assiter, Alison and Carol Avedon, eds. *Bad Girls and Dirty Pictures: The Challenge to Reclaim Feminism.* Boulder, Col. and London: Pluto Press, 1993.

Bell, Laurie, ed. *Good Girls/Bad Girls: Feminists and Sex Trade Workers Face to Face.* Seattle, Wash.: Seal Press, 1987.

Bolton, Richard, ed. *Culture Wars: Documents from the Recent Controversies In the Arts.* New York: The New Press, 1992.

Brownmiller, Susan. *Against Our Will: Men, Women and Rape.* New York: Simon and Schuster, 1976.

Burstyn, Varda, ed. *Women Against Censorship.* Vancouver. B.C.: Douglas and McIntyre, 1985.

Delacost, Frederique and Priscilla Alexander, eds. *Sex Work: Writings by Women in the Sex Industry.* Pittsburgh, Penn.: Cleis Press, 1987.

Dworkin, Andrea. *Pornography: Men Possessing Women.* New York: Plume reprint, 1989.

Ellis, J. "Photography/pornography: art/pornography." *Screen* 20 (1980).

Ellis, Kate et al., eds. *Caught Looking: Feminism, Pornography and Censorship.* F.A.C.T. Book Committee. New York: Caught Looking Inc., 1986

Hart, Linda.
"Karen Finley's Dirty Work: Censorship, Homophobia, and the NEA." *Genders* 14 (Fall 1992)

Heartney, Eleanor.
"A Necessary Transgression: In Defense of Pornography." *New Art Examiner* (November 1988): 20-23.

Hunt, Lynn, ed.
The Invention of Pornography: Obscenity and the Origins of Modernity, 1500-1800.
New York: Zone Books, 1993.

Johnson, Reed.
"Sex, Laws and Videotapes."
Detroit News (December 7, 1992): 2E

Lederer, Laura, ed.
Take Back the Night: Women on Pornography. New York: William Morrow, 1980.

MacKinnon, Catherine A.
Towards a Feminist Theory of the State. Cambridge, Mass. and London: Harvard University Press, 1989.

Nead, Lynda.
The Female Nude: Art, Obscenity and Sexuality. New York and London: Routledge, 1992.

New York Times.
"Artists, Accepting Federal Grants, Worry About Strings."
(March 10, 1990).

Patton, Cindy.
"Safe Sex In the Pornographic Vernacular." In *How Do I Look?Queer Film and Video.* Edited by Bad Object Choices. Seattle, Wash.: Bay Press, 1991: 31-63.

Patton, Cindy.
"Visualizing Safe Sex: When Pedagogy and Pornography Collide." In *Inside/Out: Lesbian Theories, Gay Theories.* Edited by Diana Fuss. New York: Routledge, 1991: 373-386.

Samaras, Connie.
"Look Who's Talking." *ArtForum* 29 (November 1991): 102-106.

Sprinkle, Annie.
Post Porn Modernist. Created by Willem de Ridder. Amsterdam: Torch Books, 1991.

Stanley, Lawrence A.
"Art and 'Perversion': Censoring Images of Nude Children." *Art Journal* 50 (Winter 1991): 21-27.

Stoller, Robert J.
Porn: Myths for the Twentieth-Century. New Haven and London: Yale University Press, 1991.

Stoltenberg, John.
Refusing to Be a Man: Essays on Sex and Justice. New York: Meridian, 1989.

Vance, Carol S.
"Feminist Fundamentalism—Women Against Images." *Art In America* 81 (September 1993): 35-39.

Vance, Carol S.
"Misunderstanding Obsenity"
Art In America 78 (May 1990): 49-55.

Vance, Carol S.
"New Threat to Sexual Expression: The Pornography Victims' Compensation Act." *SIECUS Report* (February 1992): 20-21.

Vance, Carol S.
"Photography, Pornography, and Sexual Politics." *Aperture* (Fall 1990): 52-65.

Vance, Carol S.
Pleasure and Danger: Exploring Female Sexuality. Boston: Routledge and Kegan Paul, 1984.

Vance, Carol S.
"Reagan's Revenge." *Art In America* 78 (November 1990): 49-55.

Vance, Carol S.
"The Pleasure of Looking: The Attorney General's Commission on Pornography versus Visual Images." In *The Critical Image: Essays on Contemporary Photography.* Seattle, Wash.: Bay Press, 1990: 38-58.

Vance, Carol S.
"The War on Culture." *Art In America* 77 (September 1989): 39-45.

Watney, Simon.
Policing Desire: Pornography, AIDS, and the Media. Minneapolis: University of Minnesota Press, 1987.

Williams, Linda.
Hardcore: Power, Pleasure, and the "Frenzy of the Visible." Berkeley: University of California Press, 1989.

Psychoanalysis

Charcot, Jean Martin and Georges Didi-Huberman.
Invention de l'hystéria: Charcot et l'iconographie photographique de la Salpêtrière. Paris: V. 1, 1877; V. 2, 1878; V. 3, 1879-80; revised: Paris, ·1982.

Cixous, Helene and Catherine Clement.
The Newly Born Woman.
Paris, 1975. Translated by Betsy Wing. Minneapolis: University of Minneapolis Press, 1986.

Cixous, Helene.
"The Laugh of the Medusa."
In *Modern Feminisms: Political, Literary, Cultural.* Edited by Maggie Hume. New York: Columbia University Press, 1992.

Hirsch, Marianne.
The Mother/Daughter Plot: Narrative, Psychoanalysis, Feminism.
Bloomington and Indianapolis: Indiana University Press, 1989.

Institute of Contemporary Art, ed.
Desire: ICA Documents.
London: ICA, 1984.

Kristeva, Julia.
"Giotto's Joy." In *Desire In Language: A Semiotic Approach to Literature and Art.* Edited by Leon S. Roudiez. Translated by Thomas Gora et al. Oxford, England: Basil Blackwell, 1981: 210-236.

Kristeva, Julia.
"Motherhood According to Giovanni Bellini." In *Desire In Language: A Semiotic Approach to Literature and Art.* Edited by Leon S. Roudiez. Translated by Thomas Gora et. al. Oxford, England: Basil Blackwell, 1981: 237-270.

Kristeva, Julia.
Powers of Horror: An Essay on Abjection. New York: Columbia University Press, 1982.

Lacan, Jacques.
Feminine Sexuality: Jacques Lacan and the École Freudienne.
Edited by Juliet. Mitchell and Jacqueline Rose. London: Macmillan, 1982.

Moi, Toril.
Sexual/Textual Politics: Feminist Literary Theory. London and New York: Methuen, 1985.

Moi, Toril.
The Kristeva Reader. Oxford, U.K.: Basil Blackwell Press, 1986.

Pollock, Griselda.
"Trouble In the Archives."
Women's Art Magazine 54 (September/October 1993): 10-13.

Rose, Jacqueline.
"Sexuality and Vision: Some Questions." In *Vision and Visuality.* Edited by Hal Foster. Seattle, Wash.: Bay Press, 1988.

Rose, Jacqueline.
Sexuality In the Field of Vision. London: Verso Books, 1986.

Photography Credits